FAKING
IT

FAKING IT

How to Seem Like a Better Person
Without Actually Improving Yourself

Amir Blumenfeld
Neel Shah
Ethan Trex

The Writers of CollegeHumor.com

DUTTON

DUTTON

Published by Penguin Group (USA) Inc.
375 Hudson Street, New York, New York 10014, U.S.A.
Penguin Group (Canada), 90 Eglinton Avenue East, Suit 700, Toronto, Ontario M4P 2Y3, Canada (a division of Pearson Penguin Canada Inc.); Penguin Books Ltd, 80 Strand, London WC2R 0RL, England; Penguin Ireland, 25 St Stephen's Green, Dublin 2, Ireland (a division of Penguin Book Ltd); Penguin Group (Australia), 250 Camberwell Road, Camberwell, Victoria 3124, Australia (a division of Pearson Australia Group Pty Ltd); Penguin Books India Pvt Ltd, 11 Community Centre, Panchsheel Park, New Delhi–110 017, India; Penguin Group (NZ), 67 Apollo Drive, Mairangi Bay, Auckland 1311, New Zealand (a division of Pearson New Zealand Ltd.); Penguin Books (South Africa) (Pty) Ltd, 24 Sturdee Avenue, Rosebank, Johannesburg 2196, South Africa

Penguin Books Ltd, Registered Offices: 80 Strand, London WC2R 0RL, England

Published by Dutton, a member of Penguin Group (USA) Inc.

First printing, March 2007
3 5 7 9 10 8 6 4 2

Copyright © 2007 by CollegeHumor Press, LLC
All rights reserved

🄯 REGISTERED TRADEMARK—MARCA REGISTRADA

LIBRARY OF CONGRESS CATALOGING-IN-PUBLICATION DATA HAS BEEN APPLIED FOR.

ISBN 978-0-525-94991-6

Printed in the United States of America
Set in Adobe Garamond and Futura
Designed by Jaime Putorti

Contents

Acknowledgments

We would like to extend our sincerest gratitude to Samantha von Sperling of Polished Social Image Consultants, Steve Hindy of the Brooklyn Brewery, Ethan Kelley of the Brandy Library, and Dr. Mark Schweizer for sharing his music expertise. If you should see any of these people on the street, please give them a high five. All the way up top. That's the only way to do it.

Introduction

Before you start reading this book, take a moment and think about the person you would like to be. Is this guy or gal sophisticated, witty, and resourceful? Armed with a broad array of cultural knowledge matched only by a deep well of practical know-how and an effortless charisma with the opposite sex? What would you say if there was a pill you could take that would turn you into this ideal human? Now, what would you say if this pill was too large to swallow but could easily be read, and upon completion could give you the same results as the aforementioned magical pill? Congratulations, you are now holding said pill. (Please stop eating this book, you just don't understand the metaphor yet.)

Odds are, you desire these attributes not just so you can

spice up your internal monologue with allusions to the lesser works of Sherwood Anderson or have something interesting to think about on long car trips. No, you want them so you can impress people. Show a little extra flair, and nabbing sexual partners becomes infinitely easier, right? Conspicuously displaying heightened intelligence and diligence can only score you points with your boss. A perceived passion for academic subjects and other weighty mental pursuits will earn you the respect and admiration of your professors. Are you picking up on a pattern here? The important thing isn't *who* you are; it's who other people *think* you are. Who you are is a guy who spends all of his free time at the video arcade trying to beat Cruisin' USA on one credit; but that doesn't mean others can't think you are the kind of guy who spends his lazy afternoons boning up on the finer points of midcentury modern decorative art philosophies.

Your imperative is clear then. You have to fool everyone you encounter into believing you're some sort of elevated, improved man. It sounds like lying, but it's not. Okay, that's a lie in itself, but the strategies contained in the following pages aren't designed to maliciously bend the truth. Rather, think of them as easy little ways to smooth off some of your rough edges by applying a nice soft putty of deception. Oh, that still sounds bad. Whatever—the point is these tricks will work. Much like making an omelet, if you want to impress people, you've got to break a few eggs. This adage is doubly true if you're trying to impress a young lady with your abilities as an omelet chef.

Follow our advice, and you'll start convincing people that

you know what you're doing. You'll become a guy who gets it, and others will admire you. Never again will you be forced to admit you don't actually know who Picasso is. Your days of nodding along during conversations about current events are over. Your friends will start multiplying as you become the kind of admirable Renaissance man who people want to take to parties. You'll learn how to speak intelligently on all sorts of topics at your own seemingly lavish parties that are thrown together using the money you shouldn't have earned at a job you don't necessarily deserve.

You can fake it. It's not even that hard. Trust our tips, be firm and confident, and nobody will ever know you're in completely over your head.

Being Dismissive to Hide Your Ignorance

Even if you memorize every page of this book, there will still be times when you have no idea what your conversation partners are talking about. People say there's nothing more impressive than admitting when you don't know something. They mostly say it to themselves, though, because these people have no friends. It is most impressive to be able to always speak intelligently and authoritatively about any topic that may come up.

You can't possibly be Master of All Domains, but you can certainly seem like you are. The easiest technique to achieve this effect is to be dismissive of the topic at hand. The trick here is to keep it fairly vague while using words that don't really mean anything. For example, if someone wants to discuss the importance of T. Rex's *Electric Warrior* as the best proto-glam record of all time, and you have no idea what T. Rex or glam is, keep your cool. Confidently say, "Are you kidding me? If that record were any more derivative, it would be in a calculus textbook." If your interlocutor continues to press the issue, throw out a condescending gem like, "If you can't see how obviously they crib from their influences, you should probably give it a closer listen." Now who's the asshole? This guy hasn't even listened to the record that closely, but he's arguing that it's canonical. In the arts, it's always safe to call things "reactionary"; it's pretty much a conversation stopper because art is almost by definition reactionary to something. When it comes to sports, just say that an athlete or a team has been "coached up" and isn't as good as everyone thinks. So-and-so is "just a system player." And in literature, books can be "too precious for their own good" or have characters who are "woefully flat and underdeveloped."

Why does this technique work so well? First, you're showing some courage to openly disagree with whomever you're talking to. Sitting and nodding the whole time doesn't really require any thought or guts, but disagreeing does. Second, people perceive that it takes some deeper understanding and analysis of something to dislike it. This is why music snobs hate straightforward pop music; there's nothing to analyze. If you have really given it some thought and argue that an album is derivative of its influences, then you obviously are well acquainted with not just that record, but the records of the artists who influenced it. Finally, and perhaps most importantly, the vague nature of your dismissal means that you can't be asked the kind of specific questions that reveal your lack of knowledge. If you hate something, nobody's going to ask you what your favorite part was. This method is airtight. Use it wisely, but don't break it out too often. Nobody wants to be around the guy who hates everything. Also, you'd be dead wrong about that T. Rex record . . . it fucking rocks.

How to Bait Someone into Telling You a Story

Everybody has done something impressive over the course of their life. Whether it be climbing to the top of Mount Kilimanjaro, winning a dinette set on *The Price Is Right,* or saving a stranger's life, impressive accomplishments come in all shapes and sizes. They're not worth anything to you unless you can brag about them, though.

Unfortunately, these feats of skill, bravery, or intelligence are usually too obscure to squeeze into everyday conversation. "You went shopping today? That's so weird because five years ago I made it to the round of sixteen on *American Idol*" is not a natural segue. So you'll have to be creative in order to get somebody to ask you about the time in 1991 you won a statewide spelling bee. Here are some tips:

- Get a tattoo commemorating the event: Nobody is going to ask you about the time you accidentally gave Michael Jordan the flu during the NBA finals, but they will ask you what that giant sneeze symbol on your right forearm means.

- Get a wingman: "Oh man, did you tell her about that time you won that national hot dog eating contest!?" It's not bragging if somebody else brings it up. Every night. For five bucks. All right, ten, but you gotta be more subtle about it!

- Make it an anniversary: Who cares about the exact date that you stopped that bank robbery? Nobody will second guess you when you tell them it was "ten years ago today." You may have to be careful when bringing up seasonal accomplishments, though—no one is going to believe you saw the Miracle on Ice from the fifth row during the '80 Winter Games in August.

Important Note: Regardless of which method of passive bragging you use, it's important that you express the utmost resistance: "No, please, I can't tell this elevator-baby-delivery story again, it bores me to death. I don't even know where I put the

A commemorative tattoo is a great way to induce people into asking you to recount a heroic and memorable story.

medal." Make them force it out of you. You'll not only impress people with your accomplishments but with your modesty as well.

When to Fake Things

Look, only a few pages in and you already have a few good tactics to seem smarter and more cultured than you really are. You must use them judiciously, though, or people will think you're a jackass. All of your careful work can be undone if you act like a smarty pants at the wrong time. You won't earn a reputation as a clever, deep thinker this way; you'll be known as that pedantic asshole who can't talk about normal stuff like beer or monster trucks. Thus, you must be selective when wielding your new skills.

Under no circumstances should you attempt to impress people with your wisdom at any of the following events: book-burnings; during your presidential campaign; the Scopes monkey trial following the perfection of your time machine; or within the context of any organized religion. These are all institutions or events through which a heavy current of anti-intellectualism runs. As such, if you try to flex your brainpower you will, at best, have your ass kicked. At worst, you will be burned as a witch or condemned to a fiery eternity in hell. Yeah, apparently they can do that with impunity.

Even in more everyday situations you have to be careful, so always gauge your audience. Sure, you may have a solid ninety seconds of canned discourse on the differences between Marx's and Engel's personal philosophies, but if you're talking to someone who's truly stupid, they'll be more intimidated than

impressed by this rant, particularly since they think you're referring to popular 1990s soft-rock crooner Richard Marx. In these
situations, don't show off the full range of your knowledge; the
occasional four-syllable word in conversation and your posses-
sion of a bachelor's degree will establish your mental superiority.

Of course, you'll meet lots of people who you're just naturally smarter than, even without faking it. These people will
hate you for it, so you should endeavor to be self-deprecating
and downplay your advantages. Ask your boss questions about
his inane new business plan, and act genuinely interested when
your girlfriend's dad explains that you really can make a living
having yard sales: "You just have to go get new merchandise
every day, you see. If you play it right, you'll be able to move up
to a carport sale by this time next year." You can't argue with
that kind of success, even if you did make it through college
with a 2.95 GPA, so keep your skepticism to yourself and act
impressed.

Finally, you should never, ever act smart in the presence
of people who are legitimately brilliant. Yeah, you may have
learned five talking points about Cezanne's paintings, but if the
guy sitting next to you wrote his doctoral dissertation on the ef-
fects of postimpressionists on the development of analytic cubism, you are truly, seriously fucked where you stand. You will
end up looking a hundred million times worse than if you'd
just kept quiet or asked some pointed and well-considered questions. If you are the legitimately smart guy, don't take too much
joy in humiliating these fakers, and be similarly careful when
correcting them. That guy was joking; he didn't really think the
thunder was angels bowling, asshole.

Going Too Far

Sadly, not all cultural knowledge is created equal. While showing a comprehensive grasp of the work of Raymond Carver can
be viewed as sexy, constantly referencing Noam Chomsky just
makes you sound like a pretentious tool who's only read one
book in his entire life. The following is a list of works and
artists so widely loved and discussed that you will garner no additional cred for mentioning them. They're not bad in any way;
in fact, most of them represent the pinnacle of artistic achiev-
ment. However, if you try to talk about them, you'll only be
telling people things they already know while sounding like an
asshole.

The Unbearable Lightness of Being by Milan Kundera—
A wonderful Czech novel that explores the ups and downs of
life through the travails of a surgeon, his wife, and his lover.
Certainly one of the better books out there, but not a guide to
every single existential question you might have. Young people
quote from it like it holds all the answers. Go ahead, drop one
little "Einmal ist Keinmal," the book's central phrase, but don't
come running to us when you get slapped in the face for being
a pompous prick. Really, anything that's inspired both the precious writer Jonathan Safran Foer *and* the precious band Bright
Eyes has probably exhausted its underground cache.

Radiohead—Are they arguably the greatest band in the
world? Yes. Have their records shown shocking development
and far-ranging influence? Yes. Is there a single thing you

can say about any Radiohead song, record, or show that three dozen people haven't already articulated? No. So stop trying.

Any movie written by Charlie Kaufman—*Being John Malkovich, Eternal Sunshine of the Spotless Mind,* and *Adaptation* all probably changed the way you look at film, and each one had its own little flairs that made it accessible but still "difficult." Yes, they're undoubtedly great, but if you keep harping on about them, you'll seem like that guy who latches on to one little thing that everyone already knows and pontificates on it to sound smart. You really don't want to be that guy.

Jackson Pollock—Pollock was a tremendously influential force in the world of abstract art, and his iconoclastic paintings helped shape the next several decades of art history. However, if you say he's your favorite painter, you will sound like someone who remembers one drip piece he saw as a fourth-grader on a museum tour. Never, ever challenge Pollock's greatness; you'll look like a buffoon. However, you should be hesitant to bring him up at all for fear of sounding trite.

Appropriate Body Language

Did you know that among deaf people 100 percent of communication is nonverbal? The number is high for those of us who can hear, too, so it's important to appear as confident as possible when spouting complete falsehoods, half-truths, uncertainties, and lies. Benjamin Franklin once said a lie spoken confidently rings truer than a fact spoken meekly. We just made that quote up, but if you said it firmly while leaning forward and never losing eye contact, people would believe you because you appeared articulate and poised.

Positive body language may not come naturally to you at first. But practice it with new people you meet, and soon it will become habit. There are a myriad of ways to convey confidence, but none are more important than good posture and eye contact. Standing as tall as you can and never losing eye contact is the first thing they teach at president school, and though that little "incident" in college with the eight-ball and dead hobo likely precludes the possibility that you'll one day run for office, you still want to come off as someone who could. No matter how confused you are or how little you know about something, always remember to stand tall and never lose eye contact.

While this advice is good for almost any situation, it's crucial when you're spinning a web of high-grade bullshit. You can get away with almost all of the faking techniques in this book if you appear confident, stand up straight, and lie your face off. Obviously, this complete mastery of body language is easier said than done; that's why everyone isn't a pathological liar. However, if you can master the art of looking someone in the eye and conversing about things you have no idea about, you will have successfully killed that little part of you that's known as a conscience. You can still use Jiminy Cricket as bait; who wants to fry up some delicious catfish?

Of course, there is such a thing as too much eye contact. Keep focus while you are talking, but during a silence, if you're still staring at somebody, they will think you are a murderer. That slow-motion throat-slash gesture doesn't help the situation, either. Some other no-no's include touching your face, clearing your throat, folding your arms, and yelling racial slurs at the top of your lungs (sorry, what looked charismatic and confident on Hitler doesn't always jive with today's post–WWII environment).

Your body language may accidentally offend people. For example, people may misconstrue your falling asleep with your body propped on a branch as a sign of boredom.

Bullshitting Selectively

Regardless of how many History Channel documentaries you watch, how many AP tests you aced in high school, how many books you read or box scores you memorized, it's impossible to talk intelligently about everything. Even the smartest people have holes in their knowledge that prohibit them from chiming in on all conversations. When you find yourself in a discussion about a topic you know little about—such as, say, the 1919 World Series scandal, the *Godfather* trilogy, or foreign currency—it is imperative that you don't speak foolishly and just hope nobody notices. Otherwise you'll be in for a long night of desperate backtracking: "Oh yeah, that's what I meant."

Your two options in these situations are to stay silent or ask questions, and the option you choose depends on how much of the conversation at hand is common knowledge. If people are talking about something you should know about but don't (current wars, major sports figures), you're going to want to stay silent. That way, people will just assume the conversation is too mundane for you.

But if people are talking about relatively obscure items (*MASH* the movie, West African geography, the 1984 Olympics), it's okay to seem curious. Acting genuinely interested is much better than spouting incorrect information. "Yeah, Robert DeNiro sucked in that movie. Oh, he wasn't in it? Weird, I was pretty sure he was," is much worse than "Oh really? I had no idea the USSR boycotted the '84 Olympics, why did they do that?" Modesty and curiosity go a long way, and if you pay enough attention, you'll be able to learn enough to join the next conversation, so that years from now you can tell somebody, "You had no idea the USSR boycotted the '84 games? What sort of idiot are you? I'm surprised you even found directions to get here, idiot."

Things You Shouldn't Fake

Faking your way through life is a great way to get maximum results from minimal effort, and in most cases it will work perfectly if you follow our advice. However, there are certain things you probably shouldn't fake, as they can quickly become disastrous if you don't know what you're doing. To avoid considerable embarrassment, legal fees, and potential incarceration, the following are off-limits:

- Driving stick shift. Without prior practice, driving a manual will leave you looking like a fool and cause serious mechanical damage. Instead, just tell her the truth when she asks you if you know how to drive stick. It's okay to admit your first car was a '94 Accord and not a '78 Thunderbird.

- Installing electrical wiring. Wiring done improperly has a tendency to start fires. Be a man and call an electrician. Then make him put plastic bags on his shoes so you can feel better about yourself while he helps you. Look, that Oriental rug is worth more than his dignity.

- Trick shooting. We don't care how many times that carnival worker dared you; there's no way you can shoot that apple out of your girlfriend's mouth with that crossbow. It's not worth it to risk her life for the prize of a *Finding Nemo* doll.

- Piloting a commercial airliner. "Autopilot" may make it sound easy, but there's still a lot of expertise required.

- Delivering a baby. It seemed easy on every sitcom you watched as a child, but there's more to being an emergency obstetrician than telling her to breathe and push. Furthermore, you're too young and unemployed to deal with the medical malpractice suit.

Everything else is fairly manageable with little to no expertise, so let's get started.

CHAPTER 1

Scholarly Pursuits

You probably think school is all knowledge based, so if you don't know something, you will fail. You believe that professors are trained to sniff out ignorance and punish it. Not true. At all levels of education, the smartest people never get the best grades. This leaves the door open to idiots just like yourself! While the real smart ones* sit around on the quad and talk about how much they admire Nietzsche, you can be the one at home trying to get your old Nintendo to work while pulling straight A's. That's right, you can fake your way to scholastic success, just like anything else. In fact, school may

---

*We mean the real pretentious kids, not the smartest. Yes, there are important differences. Bringing Hegel into a conversation about basketball is only one of them.

be the easiest arena to pull the wool over the eyes of the world at large.

How do you pull this particular con? Academia is perhaps the most poorly designed system in the world, but it's got too much tradition behind it to change now. A big part of this tradition is the reliance on the GPA or grade point average. Others' perception of your academic abilities are predicated almost exclusively upon the grades you've earned and, more specifically, your GPA. The GPA is handy because, like a batting average or a blood-alcohol level, it quantifies all of your achievements into a nice, tidy number. However, there's not much ground for comparison among these numbers. What's more impressive: a 4.0 at a huge party school or a 3.5 at an Ivy? Is it tougher to get good grades as a music major or a physics major? Who knows? The important thing is, your GPA will be the badge that marks how smart you are, and unless you're talking to some sort of registrar, nobody will ever know if you're fudging. Hence, from this day forward, you had a 3.62 GPA in college. If you actually did worse than that, congratulations on the upgrade. If your real GPA was higher, it's probably good to deflate it a bit; you don't want people thinking you were an egghead with no life.

Of course, this new GPA will work fine for everyday conversations, but when you apply for jobs or grad school, they're going to want to see a transcript. You might think that just opening the envelope and changing your GPA on the copy of the transcript will suffice, but these HR people and admissions officers have been around the block. They'll spot that doctored document, especially if you make the changes in purple crayon.

(We don't care if you thought it would look okay; you should have taken the extra time to find a pen!) Ergo, you'll need a way to actually bump up some of your grades. Often, this process will require using words like *ergo* in essays.

When you left for college, your dad probably told you that you'd do well if you worked hard. He was on to something, but it wasn't exactly true. You'll do well in college if it *looks* like you're working hard. Professors are human, and they just want to know that you're paying attention and doing the work. Basically, all you have to do is show up for class and occasionally go to his office hours to ask a question, and you'll probably get a B at the very minimum. Be strategic, though; when you go into office hours, make sure to ask an educated question about a topic you know very well. That way, by the time the professor's done explaining it, he'll think you really, really understand. He'll feel good about being such a wonderful teacher who can still reach young minds even in his old age, and you'll feel good because you stole ninety-four cents out of his change dish while he was explaining something on the whiteboard behind him. Time to buy some Lifesavers, sucker!

Next stop, banging that cute Romance-languages TA!

Getting Grades Raised

No matter what level of school you're in, be it undergraduate, grad school, or even law school, you're probably worrying about your grades a little more than you let on. So, what to do when you get a paper or an exam back with a low score that just won't do? Arriving at office hours on the verge of tears with a baseball bat trying to explain the GPA differential between a B+ and an A− isn't going to help. You need to act cool and try the following:

- Remember that in most classes, grades aren't determined by any sort of mathematical process. The professor looks at how you've done, incorporates your in-class participation, gauges his feelings about you, then writes down a grade. Even if you do manage to whine your way into getting three more points on the midterm or an A− rather than a B+ on your paper, the professor's going to hate you when assigning overall grades. Your chance of getting an A for the semester goes up considerably if you don't complain about every individual B. Don't complain about every bee, either. Jesus, you're allergic, and you got stung. We get it. There are other people at this picnic, too, though, and they're not all swelling up like attention whores.

- You're more likely to curry favor and persuade the professor to raise your grade if you explicitly state that you don't care about the grade when you go in to clarify what you did wrong. If you say, "I'm not really concerned about the grade, but I want to make sure I really understand the material," the prof will be impressed by your thirst for knowledge and will automatically give you a billion more points than those bastards who are coming in to say that their sentences didn't really have syntax errors. Furthermore, this helps you develop a personal connection with the professor, which means he'll think twice before nailing you with a bad grade, especially if he knows you've been trying and really care about what he's teaching.

Holding up your professor and his family inside of his apartment may get your grades raised temporarily, but you should probably try more legal methods at GPA inflation, like attending office hours.

- Twenty minutes before the professor's office hours are supposed to start, get in to his office. Jimmy open the lock and lie in wait for his arrival. When he shows up, hit him with the ol' ether rag. While he's out, find where he records the grades, and change yours. Nothing too unbelievable, but a solid string of A–'s will do. As his motionless body begins to shudder back to life, ether rag him again. Empty the dish of butterscotch on his desk into your bag, put his right index finger in his nose, and leave through the window. He'll think he had a nose-picking-related blackout and will be too embarrassed to tell anyone. When your parents are proud of your grades and buy you a bag of butterscotch as a reward, throw a fit. You've already got a whole bag full of them. Idiots.

QUICK TIP: If somebody asks you what you got on a test, convert the grade to a 200 point scale. "I got a 96!" sounds much more impressive than "I got an F−!"

A−, the Perfect Grade

At some point before, during, or after college or graduate school, someone will make an inquiry about your grades or how you did in a class. You don't want to say, "I slept the whole time and got a C, but, man, did the girl in front of me ever have a nice rack." (This is why many people do poorly in Calculus II.) Instead, make some vague lies about "doing pretty well." If they are rude and press for a grade, there's only one acceptable answer: you got an A−.

The A− is the perfect lying grade. It shows that you worked hard and had a reasonable mastery of the material. However, if anyone asks you a question you can't answer on the topic, you've got an automatic excuse for why you can't answer it. "Oh, man, I never really understood that. It's what cost me the A." Perfect.

Effectively Bullshitting on an Exam

Most professors are armed with a litany of one-liners about exams designed to inspire, motivate, or scare their students. You've heard these clichés in different forms throughout your academic career: "Just study and you'll do fine"; "This is not a difficult exam"; and "The shortest answers usually score the best because they are correct and concise."

Sometimes in the middle of a test you'll notice that the exam *is* a difficult one, you *did* study, and you're currently *not* doing fine. If you find yourself staring blankly at a question unable to decipher what it is even asking, your goal for that specific question has to change. You are no longer shooting for "correct"; you are now shooting for "better than zero."

If this is an English exam you can almost always do something that will give you some credit. Writing complete gibberish for five paragraphs will give you pity points even though you've answered the question no better than somebody who left it blank. As long as the gibberish is at least tangentially related to the topic of the class, you'll maybe swing half credit. If this is a math-based test like economics or statistics, just answer a different question entirely. It's better to answer a random question correctly than to leave the real one blank. The grader may mistake you for a smart student who misread the question, rather than a dumb one who couldn't understand what the exam was asking. Remember, you are just aiming for anything better than zero, which is what you actually deserve.

If all else fails, flip your exam over to the back and write, "George Washington Carver, ca. 1861–1943." Many of these tests are graded by TAs who aren't in the classroom when the exam is administered, so even though there wasn't an extra credit

Calculus Exam, Cont.

17) Does the equation

$$x^5 + y^5 + xy + 4 = 0$$

define an implicit function
$x = g(y)$ locally near the point
$(x,y) = (-2,2)$? Explain.

Answer:

Battle of New Orleans
January 8, 1815

When stumped on an exam, it is always better to answer a question they didn't ask than to incorrectly answer the one they did.

question, they may just give you bonus points for getting the dates right. This is doubly true for any class in your college's peanut sciences department.

Note: It's rare that your exam will be a multiple-choice one, but if it is, there is no bullshitting allowed. If you really want to bullshit, circle all five answer choices and call it a day.

QUICK TIP: If you failed an exam, try not to get too depressed. Put things in perspective. At least it wasn't a breast exam. If it *was* a breast exam, tell yourself at least it wasn't a statistics quiz.

Faking Your Way Through a Language Test

If your school requires foreign-language classes, at some point you'll probably have to take a test that has a conversation component. Usually, this is a timed exercise that involves a TA asking you some pretty simple questions in the language, and you answering. Hey, you're having a discussion in a foreign language! You can feel your confidence swelling! Let's go to Barcelona! Unfortunately, you probably aren't fluent enough to have a conversation. But fear not, you can fake your way through this, too.

- Don't answer the questions honestly. Answer with the first semi-appropriate word in the language that comes to your mind. The person you're talking to is a TA, not your mom, so they'll never know that tennis is not really your favorite sport. Now, you could even answer that your favorite hobby is lying, but you have no idea how to say "lying."

- Treat the conversation like a bad date and keep flipping the questions back at the TA. Since these tests are usually timed, your first goal should be killing the five minutes. The easiest, quickest way to do that is by answering the question, then adding *"¿y tu?"* or its equivalent to the end of your response. The TA will now have to think of an answer and articulate it, killing time while you sit there and nod. Not only have you saved yourself serious effort, but you seem like you're interested in the thoughts of your TA, who is probably a lonely, miserable grad student.

- A third, riskier option is to stare deep into the TA's eyes after the first question and declare, *"Te amo con el todo mi corazón."* Her surprised stammering should eat up at least a few minutes of the clock, and then she'll say some crap in Spanish that probably means, "I'm flattered, but no." Then she'll probably just give you an A— to get you out of the room. *¡Bueno!*

- If you can't even muster this much of your language, show up for the exam sporting a sombrero, beret, or other language-appropriate headwear. You'll still fail, but damn, you'll look authentic doing it.

QUICK TIP: Don't know Spanish fluently? Don't worry! Just learn Portuguese. They're so close, nobody will be able to tell the difference!

When taking a language test, it's important to look the part. To avoid any awkward situations, double-check that your clothes correspond with the language being tested.

Slacking on a Group Project

If you've been assigned to a group project, your options are pretty clear: You can drop out of school, ride from city to city on the rails, fighting other drifters with homemade knives, everything you own in the hobo bindle on your back, or you can buckle down and try to figure out how to get the rest of the group to do it for you.

We'd recommend the latter.

It's important to clarify one thing from the outset: If you want to be a free rider, you should have taken the hobo option, because you'll have to do *some* work in your project group. The key is figuring out how to do the minimum level to placate the group without exerting yourself. Often, this tactic involves bringing the snacks. Slicing oranges may not be any fun, but it's a damn sight better than spending four hours putting together a PowerPoint. Especially a PowerPoint about orange slices.

In this vein, it is imperative that you never, ever volunteer to do the bibliography. You may think it sounds easy. But you'll have to nag everyone to send you his references, then you'll have to figure out how to cite one Web site with four authors. Trust us, it's not as simple as it sounds. It's rumored that one paper cited a single Web site with seventy-two authors. The bibliography was longer than the Manhattan phone book and required a pack of burros to carry it.

A better strategy is to try to establish yourself as the group expert on some facet of the project. A safe bet here is to pick the most complicated part and speak in vague terms about it. The others will think you understand it better than they do, and you're set. The upside here is that the most complicated part of group work is almost always the shortest, least important, and least work intensive.

If you're too lazy to do even that, then quickly establish yourself as the "group leader" at the first meeting by trying to move discussion along. Sit quietly while tasks are divvied up, and then at the end, you'll have no job and you can volunteer to write the conclusion. Luckily for you, the conclusion requires no research and no real thought; you just paraphrase what everyone else has already said. Then, you make copies of the final product, and you're done. Great, you've just earned half of your grade in a course with an hour of work. Even the guys who write Ziggy cartoons put more time and thought into them.

There's only one last rule for group-project etiquette. You have to show up for every meeting, and you have to show up on time. One, it's polite, and two, nobody else will show up for all the meetings. You're automatically the most devoted group member, even without doing anything, and no one will point out that offering to take the final project to Kinko's to get copies made doesn't really count as a third of the work. Don't worry about those chumps; you don't need them anymore.

Faking Your Way Through a Study Date

Is there a more blatant example of misaligned intentions than the study date? You're bragging to your friends that you've got this "killer study sesh with this hottie from calc"; she's telling her friends she's "studying with some dork from class." Your basic intention for these pseudodates is to impress the girl with your monstrous intellect in an unthreatening, no-pressure context. Unfortunately, this only works if you actually know what's going on in the class. Reading that comic-book adaptation of *Oliver Twist* was a great way to spend that half hour in the bathroom, but it's not adequate preparation for your Novels of Dickens final. Now, you've got to figure out how to woo a girl while also pretending you know what happened during both the best of times *and* the worst of times. Wait, they occurred simultaneously? Crap, this is going to be harder than you thought.

Showing up for a study date without any actual knowledge doesn't mean you can't impress, though. In fact, it can even be preferable to actual knowledge in the right situations. Chances are, this girl isn't showing up to be wooed by you; she's showing up to learn all of organic chemistry in an hour while working under the assumption that anyone who looks like you must be smart. This will teach her to never judge a book by its cover, although you don't even know what the cover of the textbook looks like. You think it's brown, but you traded it for Chiclets months ago. Don't worry, this lack of knowledge is going to make you the most impressive study date in history.

You basically fake your way through this situation by continuously asking the girl questions about the topic—but make them sound like they're leading her to a well-considered test response. Instead of asking her what happens in *Macbeth,* ask, "If you were the director, what major plot points would you emphasize in your production?" She'll start filling you in on what happens, and you can base more questions off of that. Meanwhile, she will be loving it because you're really testing her knowledge on the topic and making her think on her feet. Obviously, she will assume you're already an expert on the topic if you're spending your time helping her check her understanding, so just keep asking questions that will get the basics out of her, then build on them. Some examples:

- "Compare and contrast this war with any other that we studied in class." (This question is key because it fills you in on two topics, and compare and contrast is basically just an invitation to list a bunch of facts.)

- "What do you think is the most difficult concept in the course, and how would you explain it to someone who's never encountered it before?"

- "What do you think the most probable test question is, and how would you answer it?"

- "What is your phone number and your favorite type of food? How does this compare with the New Deal?"

Perfect. You've now reinforced everything she already knew while seeming like a detached genius who didn't need the extra work. Little does she know that she taught you quite literally everything you know.

Talking Like You've Done the Reading

Okay, so when the teacher assigned pages 149–276 to be read over the weekend, it wasn't merely a suggestion. You know that now. However, 50 percent of your grade is in-class participation, so you had better start acting like you did the reading.

The most effective method is piggybacking. Piggybacking is a delicate science, whereby the idiot (you) expands on an idea that has already been made by a nerd (somebody else) who has actually done the reading.

In some ways, piggybacking is a lot like being a vulture. Instead of coming up with any original ideas about the reading you haven't done, you just wait to swoop in and explain, debunk, or agree with an idea that somebody else actually spent time constructing. In other ways, however, piggybacking is not at all like being a vulture; for example, you'll rarely, if ever, eat the flesh off a rotting buffalo carcass.

Ex 1:

> Them: "I believe the party scene with Jake and Brett truly epitomized the Lost Generation, in terms of how Hemingway structured their conversation, being extremely directionless and meandering."
>
> You: "Really? I don't think their conversation lacks direction, I just think Hemingway was trying to be as natural as possible. That's just how conversations usually are."
>
> Teacher: "Good point, You."

Let's break down what just happened. Some other person in the class read over one hundred pages of Hemingway's *The Sun Also Rises* this weekend. He took notes, formulated a hypothesis, and presented it to the class. You played Mario Kart this weekend. You waited until he was done talking, then politely disagreed, and the teacher thinks you're the better student. To put it in terms you can understand, you blasted the nerd's ass with a red turtle shell.

Piggybacking is undoubtedly useful, but it's inherently flawed: Not everybody can rely on it. Freeloading only works if there are suckers who will do the reading so you can piggyback off of them. Over the course of the semester, as people start realizing that doing the reading isn't all that worthwhile, there will invariably come a day when nobody does the reading. English teachers call it "Black Monday" regardless of what day of the week this falls on. Don't worry, all hope is not lost.

You can still employ the skim-and-speak method. This tactic involves finding a random excerpt of the reading midclass and making one quasivalid point about it to really get the ball rolling. The teacher will be so thrilled that somebody made a comment, she won't even care that it's unintelligible. She wants to believe people did the reading as much as you want her to believe it.

Ex: 2

> Teacher: "Well, didn't anybody do the reading?"
> You: "Well, on page 151, I noticed Jake was talking to himself. Maybe that means something?"
> Teacher: "Good! Good! Okay, great. I'm still doing my job well. I'm still a good teacher. There's no need to take that real estate license exam."

Takeaway Point: Just because you didn't do the reading, doesn't mean you can't participate. As we saw in example 1, if other people did the reading and participated, you can just add on to their thoughtful comment. But as we saw in example 2, if nobody did the reading, then you can just read a passage aloud. The teacher will be so thrilled that somebody is pretending to be doing the reading that she'll convince herself that you actually did it. Either way you'll get the participation credit you'll need. Next stop: Recess!

Don't forget the top three books that you can just as easily rent the movie:

3. *The Portrait of a Lady*

2. *The Adventures of Huckleberry Finn*

1. The script to *Titanic*

QUICK TIP: A picture may be worth a thousand words, but that doesn't mean that finishing one issue of *X-Men* is equivalent to reading *War and Peace.*

The Magic of Having a Library Card

Of all the things that can accidentally fall out of your wallet, a library card is possibly the most impressive. As unlaminated pieces of paper go, it's way more useful than a Social Security card if you're trying to get laid (unless your target is desperate for American citizenship and/or a small old-age pension). At first it may seem counterintuitive, because having both the interest and the financial wherewithal to actually buy books would seem more impressive. Think again. Toss out a little line like, "Yeah, Amazon's good, but sometimes you just want to read a Dos Passos novel that's been out of print since the 1940s. What, you haven't read *Adventures of a Young Man* lately?" Having a library card says that you know so much about books and are so passionate about reading that the average bookstore is ill-suited to sate your passion. And that's impressive, even if you just went to look at books of "artistic" nudes or bad movies on VHS. Where else can you keep *Ishtar* for an entire week and not pay for it? Really, it's the thinking-man's Hollywood Video.

Lying About Where You Went to College

There are only so many spots available for freshmen in the Ivy League and its equivalents; therefore, way more people went to crummy colleges than good ones. Just playing the percentages, that probably means you went to a university that wasn't break- ing the front page of the *U.S. News & World Report* college rankings. Fear not, for you can get out of this situation with a smart spot of faking that those privileged New England jerks would never have dreamed of. Nor would they have to. They pay people to dream of things for them.

- If you went to a small school of dubious quality in a state where the large state university is a great school, save yourself embarrassment and several minutes of explain- ing where it was by just saying the name of the state. "Where did you go to college?" "North Carolina." Not only is it true, but people will think you went to a much more prestigious institution like the University of North Carolina at Chapel Hill. Suckers.

- Mumble. You would be surprised at how a little poor enunciation can shoot your way up the ladder of academic prestige. Hartford becomes Harvard, Lake Forest becomes Wake Forest, and the Overpass Vocational and Technological Institute becomes Yale! Again, you're not technically lying to them; their ears are.

You may have to make an online order, but people are more willing to believe you went to Harvard if you actually wore a Harvard sweatshirt. It's well worth the cost of shipping.

- Let your clothes speak for you. Wearing a shirt from a well-known bastion of intellectualism can be the only statement you need. When someone says, "Oh, wow, you went to Cal Tech?" respond with "Well, I couldn't very well buy this shirt on eBay for fourteen bucks with another seven for shipping from a seller who prefers PayPal, could I?" If they answer no, they'll be the dumb one; that's exactly what you did. You've already gotten the positive feedback from both of them, though.

Getting Tenure at an Ivy League School

There's one sure-fire way to broadcast that you are an academic giant who knew what he was doing in school: Become a professor. For most people, becoming a tenured professor at an Ivy League school is a journey that takes over a decade. Not for you, though. You're going to be a professor by the end of this article. Here's how:

1. Throw away all of your clothing. Replace it with tweed. Tweed everything. Socks, underwear, belts, gym shorts . . . if it's not tweed, it doesn't touch your body.

2. Buy a pipe that you can suck on pensively. Walk to your local college campus, locate its quadrangle, or "quad" for short, and stroll around with one hand behind your back, the other holding your pipe. Approach students on the quad and offer some professorial advice like "No, no, you forgot to add a constant of integration to the end of that

expression." They won't know what that has to do with ultimate Frisbee right now, but they'll get it later.

3. Once you feel comfortable with this system, it's time to start teaching. Many animals just assume the first creature they see is their mother. Similarly, most college students will assume whoever shows up on the first day of class is

To achieve tenure at an Ivy League university you will need to act the part, so purchase a tweed hoody and pipe. Looking good!

the professor. Arrive a few minutes early, stroll to the front of the room, and say, "Okay, okay, people, settle, settle. Come on now. Immanuel Kant's not going to debate himself." When the real professor shows up, no Harvard doctorate or campus security officer armed with pepper spray will be enough to take your authority from you. "Your first assignment is to tackle that imposter!"

4. After you pull this maneuver seven or eight semesters in a row, the university will be ready to admit defeat. You'll get a cushy endowed professorship with a corner office and personal assistant. Sit back in that big leather desk chair, pop open a copy of *Cracked,* and enjoy your standing as a mental giant.

CHAPTER 2

Arts and Culture

Even if the closest you've ever been to a library or a conservatory is playing a rousing game of Clue with your great aunt, in the study, with a candlestick, you can still seem like a cultured individual. Culture, whether popular or highbrow, is a crucial component of seeming like an improved person. It is the default conversational chatter for cocktail parties, dinners, and that awkward moment after a lap dance when the waitress asks you if you want to buy the stripper a drink.

Cultural conversation is basically the thinking-man's version of talking about the weather; people fall back on it when they've got nothing else to say. How many times has a date been going poorly, so you asked her what her favorite book was? And how many times has she said *Bridget Jones's Diary,* causing you to fake food poisoning so you could go home early? Probably a lot. These questions are escape hatches for dying conversations because they're so easy; everyone has a favorite movie. There are no wrong answers, except for *Speed 2: Cruise Control.* Plus, people are always in a good mood if they're talking about their favorite things. Asking a question about someone's aesthetic tastes can never fail.

However, if you want to really seem like a cultured person, you can't just ask the question. You also have to be ready and able to follow up on whatever she says. So if she loves Chekhov, you're not going to look any smarter by saying, "Oh, is he Czech, or did he just enjoy completing his to-do list?" And she's definitely not going to sleep with you now. But if you knew that Chekhov wrote *The Cherry Orchard,* you could take that one little fact and swing the conversation back to more familiar ground like, "Ah, *The Cherry Orchard.* That reminds me . . . you know what my favorite Froot Loop is? Cherry. Well, technically, I guess it's just red, but you get the picture. What's yours?" Great, you've turned a potentially ruinous conversation about Russian drama into one about breakfast cereal, an arena in which your expertise is considerably greater.

Gathering even this much knowledge can be intimidating, though, so keep a few things in mind. First, to fake your way through these conversations, you don't need to know everything. It's not a college English exam, so nobody's going to ask you what happened on page 97 of Upton Sinclair's *The Jungle.* If you know it's about the meat industry and that it's gross, you've got way more than enough knowledge to get through a few minutes of conversation. Same with *The Portrait of a Lady* and a lady and, to a lesser extent, the Bible and this Jesus character. With music, you can always get by just saying that a band either rocks or doesn't rock hard enough for you. Even if you're talking about a hard-rocking band and get called out for saying they don't bring the heat, you can just qualify: "Compared with what I listen to, they're a buncha pussies." Then throw out some made-up metal-band names that are your favorites. (We suggest Bloody Gums.) People will assume you just really like to search for obscure music and thus know more than they do.

See, it's not so hard. You just have to have basic knowledge of a lot of things with no real depth required. Just react the same way in every situation, and you're sure to make it through. Look at a painting, point to some minute detail, and wonder if it's influenced by Monet (it wasn't). Listen to someone talk about how much she loves Sleater-Kinney, then say you've always thought they rocked harder than their reputation indicated (they did). Hear that someone's favorite novel ever is *Jurassic Park* and punch him in the face (good call). Before long, you'll have a reputation as a Renaissance man with a wide-ranging cultural vocabulary. Little will people know you learned almost everything from pop-culture references in *The Simpsons*.

Do You Freelance for a Magazine? Now You Do!

One of the easiest lies to tell people is that you freelance for a magazine. Actual freelance writers don't spend very much time writing and often receive no credit once the magazine comes out.

Go out to the magazine stand and buy some intellectual peri-
odicals (note: she won't care that you freelance for *MAD*, regardless of how long it takes to make those fold-ins) and lay
them around the house. Thumb through them looking for any
small, unaccredited articles or graphics—most magazines will
have top-ten lists or something of that sort. Tear that page out
and leave it somewhere noticeable. When somebody asks you
why there are torn pages of *The Atlantic Monthly* lying around
your house, tell them that you can't stand to read magazines
with your writing still in them because "it diminishes my opinion of the publication."

Now they think you are intelligent and humble, instead of
stupid and deceptive. Not bad for an hour's work.

QUICK TIP: If somebody asks you what was the last book you
read, don't ask them to specify, "Myself, or a book that was
read to me?"

Seeming Well-Read

Reading a lot of big, important books is a sure-fire sign of someone whose mind works at a higher level than that of the general
population, most of whom are still Choosing Their Own Adventure. Unfortunately, reading takes a lot of time that could otherwise be spent watching television, having sex, or not reading. So
you'd think that only people who have actually read books could
seem well-read. But in reality, it's pretty easy to seem well versed
in all sorts of literature without much effort. Don't worry if you
run into an English major; most of them only chose it to try to

get into law school and didn't pay much attention in class. Here's a quick rundown of what you need to know:

You can forget anything that comes before roughly 1800. This stuff is good in an English-seminar kind of way, but no one's ever really going to want to talk to you about *The Canterbury Tales.* If you meet someone who does, run and be careful not to trip over their billowing pantaloons. Start instead with the easy stuff that can come up frequently. *Moby-Dick* is an incredibly difficult book to read, but you know the thrust of it: an allegory about revenge involving a whale. Talk about the long, boring discursions into technical descriptions of whaling, and joke that "Melville could have used an editor, but at least I know how to render blubber into lamp oil now." Everyone knows *The Scarlet Letter,* but no one has the balls to say that it's one-dimensional and boring. Shouldn't there be a little more nuance, like in Hawthorne's better works? Great, that ended that conversation.

After Hawthorne and Melville, a lot of stuff happens, none of which you need to remember except for *Tom Sawyer* and *Huckleberry Finn.* People who haven't read many books consider these to be the greatest American novels. They're not, although they're accessible. Interesting side note: *Tom Sawyer, Huckleberry Finn,* and *Uncle Tom's Cabin* are the three novels that everyone talks about like they've read, but they haven't. If you can remember large portions of the movies about any of these books, you're in the clear.

After the Civil War, nothing of much note happened either, as everyone was too busy thinking of new ways to oppress blacks to have time to write anything worth reading. Henry

James snuck in there with some pretty good books, but then the *twentieth* century is rife with authors you should know. Here's how to take care of most of them:

Joyce—Great drunk considered the greatest writer of the century. No one's really read his books, particularly *Ulysses,* because the prose is so dense with allusions and semisensical stream of consciousness that it can't be followed. Your opinion of him is that he's overrated, and if anyone challenges you, ask them how *Ulysses* ends. That will shut them up.

Fitzgerald—Great drunk who wrote *The Great Gatsby.* He wrote a few other good novels (particularly *Tender Is the Night*) and some wonderful stories, but he flamed out pretty early on. Say that such a waste of talent is too heartbreaking to comment on, and move the conversation in a direction with which you're more comfortable, like XBox Golf.

Hemingway—Great drunk who wrote *The Sun Also Rises*, *For Whom the Bell Tolls,* etc. Woefully misogynistic and speculated to have been gay. You can get away just knowing that his characters are all he-men and his sentences were short and to the point. This style could be considered reactionary to the more experimental prose of his contemporaries like Faulkner and Joyce. In fact, say that. Is it true? Dunno, but it sounds convincing.

Nabokov—Russian immigrant who wrote in four languages, studied butterflies, and wrote *Lolita,* which caused an international stir for its overtones of teen-fucking. If anyone mentions him, point out that *Lolita* is the most misunderstood novel of the twentieth century and that it's a study of American culture, not a love story about a guy fucking a little girl. That's just an added bonus!

Kerouac—Kerouac is a hack, read mostly by pretentious eleventh-graders and not-very-smart people who hang out in coffee shops. Don't fall into this trap, don't talk about him as a serious literary figure, and don't subject people to cringe-worthy memorized passages from *Big Sur*. The same goes triple for Allen Ginsberg.

Steinbeck—Steinbeck wrote depressing stories about poor peo-ple, mostly in California. Everyone read *Of Mice and Men* in ninth-grade English, so don't think you're going to win any points for referencing it.

Vonnegut—Vonnegut writes funny science fiction that often reads like a highbrow version of a *Simpsons* Halloween spe-cial. He's easy to read, interesting, and entertaining. You're not going to win any huge points by saying *Slaughterhouse-Five* is the most important book ever written, but showing an appreciation of *Cat's Cradle* indicates that you don't take yourself too seriously. Just say you really, really want some ice-nine.

If anyone brings up a contemporary book, say, "Nothing good's been written since *Ulysses*," and wave your hand dismissively.

This isn't true, but it will end conversation as people sit in awe of your ability to finish *Ulysses*.

QUICK TIP: Reading a book may take weeks, but rabbit-earing every forty pages takes minutes. You do the math.

Wars You Should Know

In life, you'll need some basic knowledge about famous wars to prevent you from seeming like an idiot in front of your girlfriend's ex-boyfriend. Until *Schoolhouse Rock* is bold enough to tackle these conflicts, here is a quick refresher course.

Hundred Years' War (1337–1453)

Who versus Who: England versus France

Result: French victory

Fun Fact: The Hundred Years' War lasted longer than one hundred years and wasn't really a war. It was just a series of conflicts that occurred off and on from 1337 to 1453.

Revolutionary War (1775–1783)

Who versus Who: American revolutionaries versus Great Britain

Result: America won

Fun Fact: It is believed that more Americans fought on the British side as Loyalists than on the American side. Similar speculation exists about the Spice Girl Rebellion of 1998.

War of 1812 (1812–1814)

Who versus Who: United States versus Great Britain

Result: Stalemate

Fun Fact: Francis Scott Key immortalized the first rockets used in America in the lyrics to our very own national anthem. If he knew how boring it would be before sporting events, he probably would have shortened it.

American Civil War (1861–1865)

Who versus Who: North (Union) versus South (Confederacy)

Result: Union victory

Fun Fact: Two-thirds of all related deaths were caused by disease. The other third came from boredom while watching Ken Burns's Civil War documentaries.

World War I (1914–1918)

Who versus Who: Allied Powers (Great Britain, France, Italy, Russia, and United States) versus Central Powers (Austria-Hungary, Bulgaria, Germany, and Ottoman Empire)

Result: Allied victory

Fun Fact: American GI's were called "doughboys," but their canned cinnamon rolls sucked. They made hilarious giggling noises when bayonetted, though.

World War II (1939–1945)

Who versus Who: Allied Powers (Soviet Union, Great Britain, France, United States, etc.) versus Axis Powers (Germany, Italy, Japan, etc.)

Result: Allied victory

Fun Fact: The Nazi-adopted symbol of the swastika was actually an ancient Hindu symbol for peace. They kind of ruined it for all those Indians who now had to put up different paintings.

Korean War (1950–1953)

Who versus Who: South Korea and United Nations (featuring United States, Great Britain) versus North Korea (featuring China, Soviet Union)

Result: Stalemate

Fun Fact: Dr. Seuss wrote *Green Eggs and Ham* after being challenged by his editor to produce a book using fewer than fifty different words. This isn't about the Korean War but will impress people nonetheless.

Vietnam War (1954–1975)

Who versus Who: South Vietnam, USA, South Korea, Thailand versus North Vietnam (with some help from China and the USSR)

Result: North Vietnam victory

Fun Fact: USA withdrew from the war in 1973, two years before the war technically ended, keeping our winning streak intact!

QUICK TIP: Having creative ideas and sharing them can score you serious points, but you have to stop pitching your modernized version *The LiveJournal of Anne Frank.*

Classical Music: What to Know

When attempting to appear knowledgeable about classical music, it is important to remember one thing: Only a very small percentage of the population in the United States can converse intelligently about this subject, and chances are, you're not going to run into them. Most of the small amount of peripheral knowledge that the average person has gleaned has been picked up in a freshman 8:00 A.M. Music Appreciation 103 class. Anyone who remembers anything more than the absolute basics from that class is no one you'd be talking to in public anyway.

The exceptions to the rule are people who majored or minored in music or those who actually enjoy the classics—but these individuals are few and far between, and even they can be fooled by a well-turned phrase and a little knowledge.

All classical music falls into two categories:

- Vivaldi's *Four Seasons*

- Not Vivaldi's *Four Seasons*

Vivaldi's *Four Seasons* is an orchestral composition of indeterminate length written in 1726. All other classical music falls into historic classifications that mirror the history of art (give or take fifty years).

It is not necessary to remember the dates. No one remembers them and no one cares, but there are certain characteristics about each period that you will find helpful.

Medieval—This is music written by monks since they were the only ones who could write. Don't worry about it.

Renaissance—This music sounds like the music you'd hear in a Robin Hood movie when everyone goes into the great hall for the banquet right before Robin attacks the sheriff and the big fight scene starts. It's being played by those guys in the corner wearing tights and holding weird-looking instruments. There was a lot of choral music written in the Renaissance as well, but it's all in Latin. Ignore it.

Baroque—Literally extravagant, complex, or bizarre. Most of the composers of the Baroque were writing nothing more than elevator music to be played in the ornate palaces of the aristocracy. This musical era culminates with Bach (1685–1750). There are many people (as well as musical scholars) who revere the music of Bach and can make a strong case that he is the greatest composer of all time. Bach's music is almost perfect in its symmetry and gives the listener a sense of being "mathematical." It's not, but saying so will give you an aura of semi-authority in circles of musical cretins.

Fact: Bach had twenty-one children, many of whom became composers as well.

Good Exit Line: "There hasn't been any real music written after 1750." (This will set you up as a Bach aficionado, but by saying it as you leave, it's not open to debate.)

The other Baroque composer worth noting is George Frideric Handel (1685–1759). Handel, unlike Bach, was an entrepreneur. He made several fortunes by inventing (and then supplying the music for) extravagant musical fads for a bored London society who wished they were Italians (linguine alfredo for supper is always preferable to spotted dick). Handel is known chiefly for a couple of sets of instrumental pieces (*Water Music* and *Fireworks Music*) and for his oratorios (large choral works with a story), the most famous being *Messiah*. This is pretty much the same career path Alvin and the Chipmunks followed.

Fact: *Messiah* is the only musical work to be in continuous performance (every year) since it was written in a twenty-four-day composing flurry in 1741. He gave all the proceeds to an orphanage, which squandered them on gruel.

Good Exit Line: "Handel! What a hack!" (It's a good line, because he was a hack! He stole from nearly everyone in the Baroque era, although he did so unapologetically and with aplomb.)

Classical—Three words. Wolfgang Amadeus Mozart. He died young (thirty-five years old) and many theories have sprung up as to the mysterious circumstances of his death. Although he almost certainly died of natural causes (and bad medical care), it's always good to throw a few names into any Mozart conspiracy conversation. Salieri (Mozart's rival composer) is an obvious choice, but mentioning Franz Hofdemel (Mozart's lodge brother) will raise more than a few eyebrows. Here's the story: Mozart was having an affair with Hofdemel's wife. On the day after Mozart's funeral, Hofdemel slit his pregnant wife's throat with a razor (she survived) and then slit his own throat (he didn't). Magdalena Hofdemel subsequently named her son after

Mozart. Again, similar to the bizarre end of Alvin and the Chipmunks.

Romantic—This period is characterized by music that provoked an emotional response in the listener. It's written chiefly by dead German men in tuxedos.

Fact: Beethoven was deaf at the end of his career. This did not stop him from writing the worst string quartets in the history of music.

Modern—Modern music is defined as music you can't listen to. If you are at any kind of upscale party or gathering, you will eventually have to deal with Philip Glass. He is one of the minimalist composers who make an enormous amount of money writing the same four notes over and over. Do not be tricked into going to a Philip Glass concert. If you must go, do not take a handgun. Someone will be killed, and you'll have to go to prison.

Things to remember:

When asked your opinion of the greatest composer of all time, always go with Bach or Mozart. Either choice is arguable and will hold you in good stead. You can't be effectively debated and if someone tries, simply reply "Mozart/Bach! There's nothing more to say!"

The three B's are Bach, Beethoven, and Brahms. Ignore Brahms. All well-cultured people do.

If driven into a conversation on twentieth-century music, you may make a reference to the second movement of Gorecki's

Symphony no. 3. (It's the movement with the soprano.) Whatever you do, don't be tricked into listening to the whole thing! This recording was, at one time, the best-selling CD in the history of classical music—which means it sold approximately one-tenth as many copies as Weird Al's *Alapalooza*.

Finally, always make fun of Pachelbel's Canon. Always.

The Cultural "Others": Opera and Ballet

Now that you know how to seem like you know what you're doing at the major cultural events, it's time to run through the junior varsity of high culture: opera and ballet. These two aren't as useful, but most people know next to nothing about them, so it's not hard to seem comparatively well versed. Since the bar is pretty low, here's all you need to know:

Opera—Opera is so unpopular among the general population that simply taking a girl to see one is a huge sign of your sophistication. Staying awake for the duration of the performance, while no mean feat, elevates her esteem to an even higher level. If you can make a reasonably astute comment when leaving the theater, there's a chance you'll have sex in the car on the way home. To make this comment, simply use the following terminology: Instead of talking about the words or the story, refer to the "libretto," the proper opera term for it. Whenever the performers stop singing back and forth in a dialogue and switch over to longer, melodic compositions sung by one person, it's usually an aria. Such an aria will be easy to pick out; remember it and praise it for being "breathtaking" when you're leaving. There is a 99.99 percent chance that she will think you know infinitely more about opera than she does, and you will be set.

Ballet—Ballet is God's way of saying: "You thought opera was boring? Oh, I'll show you boring." To put this statement in perspective, this guy invented church, and even He thinks ballet is boring. As with opera, you're going to get most of your points just for taking a date to something nonstandard and staying awake. Praise the grace of the performers or call the choreography "daring." This statement doesn't mean a whole lot, but what the hell are you going to say about a bunch of dancing ladies without sounding like an ass? If you're really clever, you'll segue back to something more

You can sleep throughout the opera, and your date will still appreciate the gesture. Just make sure to wake up at the end so she does not have to go home by herself.

concrete, like how Degas used to do impressionist paintings of Parisian dancers. Beyond that, just stay awake, praise the performance and the choreography in vague terms, and you'll be "the most mature, sophisticated guy" she's ever met at Hooters.

Art History—What to Know

Ever notice how any museum you go to has about a million paintings, and they all look pretty much the same to you? Don't worry, all but a select few members of the population feel the same way. This ignorance means that if you brush up on art history, even just a little, you'll automatically hurdle your way past all those chumps who took a single art class in college to fulfill a requirement. Fucking chumps.

For all practical purposes, whenever someone tries to talk to you about Art with a capital A, they're referring to something you'd see on the walls in one of these museums. For even more practical purposes, they're probably talking about something Picasso spent twenty minutes on when he really wanted some extra money to buy a jet ski.

The first recorded art was mostly painted on the cave walls in Spain and France. Not surprisingly for people who were mostly worried about not being gored by bulls or eaten by dinosaurs, most of this art is fairly unimpressive to the modern viewer. But, hey, you gotta start somewhere.

For the next several thousand years, not a whole lot of interesting stuff happened. Ancient civilizations like the Greeks and Persians made all sorts of art, particularly pottery and sculpture.

These artifacts will all look pretty much the same to the un-trained eye, so you don't need to worry about them.

Soon, painters were sitting around scratching their heads. They'd painted all the horses and cattle in the entire land, and they were flat out of ideas for subjects. Then, God sent them a gift: Jesus. Sure, it was nice of Him to redeem humanity for its sins, but Christ did even more for the painting industry. For the next fifteen hundred years or so, anyone who ran out of ideas could just whip up a picture of the nativity or the cruci-fixion and cash a check. It was a pretty sweet deal for everyone involved.

By around the start of the Gothic period in the thirteenth century, more paintings of rich people standing around and scenes of peasant life had started to pop up, although Baby Jesus was still the poster that everyone had on his dorm room's walls.

In the fifteenth century, the Renaissance started, and it brought genius artists like Leonardo and Bruneschelli with it. These guys were basically the Beatles of art history, and if you can only remember one, stick with Leonardo. Everyone knows his work, but you can talk about how he pioneered sfumato shading, which leaves a smoky haze around objects (obvious in *Mona Lisa*). If that doesn't impress whoever you're talking to, discuss his dual mastery of chiaroscuro, which uses contrasts between light and dark to make images more striking. Such technical knowledge should establish your expertise, and if any-one asks about Michelangelo, wave your hand and dismissively say, "Look, I'm not here to talk about painters you learned about watching those martial-arts turtles." Wow, you're a jerk.

Gradually, painters and, more important, their patrons started to get tired of all this religious iconography and started drifting further afield. The art was still more pretty than interesting to the uninitiated viewer, but it developed in subtle ways. The Romantics of the late eighteenth and nineteenth centuries showed an almost mystical interest in nature and used it as settings for many of their paintings. Hazy, gentle landscapes by guys like Corot or the Hudson River School are good examples of Romanticism. They were in direct opposition to the realist movement that took less of an editorial tone and presented nature and other subjects as they were. As such, realist works often depict nature as unforgiving and relentless. Here's a good way to remember the distinction:

Romanticism—Guy dancing with a bear.
Realism—Guy being devoured by a bear.

After these movements, modern art as we think of it was born. This is where things start to get tricky. Monet, Degas, Renoir, and their associates are most associated with the impressionist movement. They painted in soft, fuzzy focus in pretty colors, mostly pictures of landscapes, ballet dancers, or scenes of French life. At this point, impressionists look pretty boring, almost like something you would see on an old lady's wall calendar. However, in their day, they were considered daring rebels on the fringe of the art world, to the point at which people were literally laughing at them. The impressionists got the last laugh, though, as their paintings routinely sell for tens of millions of dollars and are favorites of college girls for dorm posters. How edgy and inspired!

After this point, Picasso starts to loom pretty large over the first half of the twentieth century. He was probably one of the most prolific artists of all time; you'll notice that every art museum you go to, no matter how small, has a half dozen of his works. High points to remember include his analytic cubist works, synthetic cubism, and his blue and rose periods, so creatively named for their dominant colors. Low points include inspiring some of the worst Counting Crows' lyrics of all time. If anyone asks you about him, say that Picasso was short. That's about it.

After Picasso, you just need to remember a few other big personalities in modern art. Jasper Johns painted American flags, targets, and the occasional bronze beer can in a flat, two-dimensional style. Jackson Pollock dripped paint on huge canvases. Mark Rothko put squares of one color on a field of another. Described like this, they all sound pretty stupid, but go to an art museum and have a look at them. You'll like it! The only thing you need to say about modern art is that you like the way it challenges the dominant historical aesthetic. Does this statement mean anything? No, but it makes you sound like you know what you're talking about and like you know what the dominant historical aesthetic would have been. Great, now go have sex in the museum's coat-check room.

QUICK TIP: "My five-year-old cousin could draw that!" isn't an appropriate critique when you're examining the arts and crafts room at the children's hospital.

How to Act in a Museum

Art museums make fantastic, cheap dates, but the express train to looking cultured and getting laid can quickly get derailed if you don't display proper museum behavior. It's not hard, though. Here's what you do:

- Stand and look thoughtfully at each painting. Cock your head ever so slightly. Walk from side to side to take it in at different angles. Get up close to feign appreciation for the brushwork and layering of paints. Don't get too close; you'll get paint on your nose.

- When you get close to the painting, say "Hm!" to no one in particular. If your date asks you what's so interesting, call the brushwork "brave." That doesn't really make any sense, but unless your date is a painter or an art history major, you'll sound like an expert. Quickly walk to the next painting before any conversation can break out.

- Don't look at abstract modern art and say, "My kid could do that!" Not only could your kid not make a Cy Twombly work, you shouldn't be advertising that you have an illegitimate child while you're on a date.

- Talk about things such as composition, color, and light. If you don't know what to say, call a painting "playful," a great vague term for anything that's not overwhelmingly depressing.

- Read the little information card next to the painting before she notices and explain the painting to her as it does on the card. Then pretend to notice the informational card and say, "Oh yeah, see, they talk about it right here. Though their date is off. He painted this in 1873, not 1874." The only date that's going right tonight is the one you're on.

- We can't stress this point enough: Don't get aroused when looking at a nude. It will totally show through those pants.

Faking an Opinion

If there is a movie or TV show you haven't seen, but you don't want to seem out of touch, just tell the person asking you that you have indeed seen what he/she is talking about, and you found it to be "hit or miss."

"Hit or miss" is the ultimate agreeable opinion because regardless of what pop culture entity you're referring to, some parts of it will be good and some will be bad. If they ask you a follow up question like "Really? Which part didn't you like?" just say something like "What are you, a detective? If you are, here's a crime for you: Man murders friend for being a nosy dick!" That should change the subject quite nicely.

Talking About Philosophy and Jazz

"You know, that reminds me of something Spinoza once said . . ." Stop right there, please. You might think that casually dropping the names of great philosophers into your standard conversations will make you sound like an urbane thinker.

Instead, it makes you sound like an asshole or a philosophy major (often one and the same). Nobody wants to hear about what Kierkegaard would have thought about Radiohead, and Heidegger probably didn't say anything relevant about what toppings you should get on your pizza. Philosphical conversations were fantastic when you were a stoned freshman hanging out in the dorms, but in the real world of paying rent and going to work, nobody wants to debate the existence of objective reality. Chances are pretty good that the only person who cares about this "totally deep" philosophical rant you're on is you, so cut the Kant and talk about something that interests everyone, like the weather.

Same goes for jazz. Starbucks and shitty faux–speakeasy bars may have tricked you into thinking otherwise, but you should never, ever make guests listen to jazz, go to a jazz bar, or discuss jazz. The only reason jazz has any pseudointellectual caché is that it's not popular. It's not popular for a reason: It's fucking boring. Don't go whining about how great it is to watch some sax player do an improv jam for twenty minutes at some shitty club. Nobody wants to be friends with some poseur who pretends to like jazz as a means of impressing people, so don't be this jerk.

Faking Foreign Travel

When done sparingly, talking about travel is everything that talking about your job isn't: engaging, entertaining, and generally enjoyable to all those within earshot. Moreover, people who travel are generally conferred with silly adjectives such as *refined* and *cultured,* even though all they really did was try to fuck drunk Australian tourists and buy shitty drugs in areas their Lonely Planet guidebooks described as "roughneck." Of course, you don't actually have to have been somewhere to talk it up—as long as the place is obscure enough, no one's gonna call bullshit. Here are five anecdotes you can throw out anywhere from cocktail parties to dates. Keep 'em brief, though. Getting caught lying is embarrassing, and if you go on too long, you might as well be your great-aunt Irene with her vacation slides from the time she got sunburned in the Florida Keys, except with fewer chins.

Africa: No one has ever been here, so you have free rein to riff on pretty much anything. Safaris are always a good bet—they highlight what everyone loves about Africa (the animals) and gloss over everything people don't (mind-numbing levels of poverty, violent crime, AIDS, Ebola, and genocide, to name the top five). When conversation shifts to the passing away of a famous politician/actor/musician/friend's mother, simply say, "So I was on a safari in the Serengeti National Park in Tanzania and had the good fortune of watching a cheetah take down a gazelle. The way it sunk its teeth into the poor creature's jugular, and refused to let go until its writhing body was lifeless, really drove home the permanent line between life and death." Then put down your drink, look around, and wait for someone to comment on how poetic you are.

Asia: Unless you're fraternizing with a bunch of i-bankers, refrain from mentioning the whirlwind underage sex tour you went on that started in Bangkok and ended with you queuing up for antibiotics at a walk-in clinic in Saigon. Much better to talk about all the youngsters being (figuratively) fucked in Cambodian sweatshops. Next time you're at Green Party fundraiser, use this line: "I don't know what all the fuss is about—I would have killed to get my hands on a pair of new-edition Air Jordans when I was nine, ha ha." Silence? Follow with "What, you think they'd rather do math problems all day long like not-poor Asians?" and you're golden. We're assuming this is one of the few racist Green Party fundraisers.

South America: People are sick of hearing about the rain forest—the sooner everyone comes to terms with the fact that it won't exist in ten years, the better. Instead, drop some esoteric cultural knowledge on them: "Did you know that they actually speak Portuguese in Brazil, and not Spanish? Maybe that's why my gardener didn't say hi back when I waved and said, *'Hola.'*"

Australia: Dingoes, kangaroos, koalas, Nicole Kidman, blah blah blah. Might as well be the Great Barrier to "Who Gives a Shit?" Next!

Europe: What, did you smoke dope and drink absinthe in Amsterdam? Do X with a bunch of German Eurotrash at a rave in Ibiza? Drink tons of twenty-five-cent Czech beer in Prague? You and every other postgrad who went to Europe to find himself on Daddy's dime. Better to avoid the continent altogether than risk sounding like a clichéd loser. And stop calling bars "pubs" when you get back. They're fucking bars, you anglophilic asshole.

Traveling the world can cost thousands of dollars. Instead, spend some money on travel gear and memorize fake stories to tell people you meet.

What Your Favorite Things Aren't

People are forever asking you what your favorite book, movie, or record are. While these choices are a matter of personal preference, we know what they definitely shouldn't be.

Not Your Favorite Book: *The Da Vinci Code*
Not Your Favorite Movie: *The Da Vinci Code*
Not Your Favorite Record: *The Da Vinci Code* Original Motion Picture Soundtrack; *The Da Vinci Code* audiobook (tie)

Ten Religions on One Page

RELIGION	WORSHIPS	GIST
Catholicism	God / Jesus / Holy Spirit	The popular one. Pope / saints / exorcisms
Protestantism	God / Jesus / Holy Spirit	The other white religion. Many denominations.
Islam	Allah	Not all Muslims are terrorists, but all squares are rectangles.
Buddhism	Buddha	They believe in karma, so break up with them at your own risk.
Judaism	God	Jews love three things: Israel, Steven Spielberg, and holidays.
Hinduism	Polytheistic	They believe in reincarnation, so no laughing when she says she hasn't been ice skating in 350 years.
Atheism	Nothing	Ironically enough, all atheists have a holier-than-thou attitude.
Pantheism	Everything	Even this book is God, so don't throw it down in disgust.
Narcissism	You	You're so vain. You probably think this gist is about you. Don't you?
Scientology	Tom Cruise	Any religion that's younger than 1,000 years old is only for crazy people.

CHAPTER 3

Jobs and Money

She works hard for the money, but that certainly doesn't mean you have to. Successfully faking it at work can significantly increase your quality of life; nothing's more satisfying than taking a nap under your desk while everyone else fiddles with spreadsheets or completes the organ-transplant surgery you were supposed to do. The stakes can be considerably higher at work than in other spheres of your life, though. If a girl finds out you're faking it on a date, she'll just decline your offer of a second date, but if your boss realizes you didn't actually go to dental school, you'll probably get fired or go to jail. Seriously, did you think just watching those old Timmy the Tooth videos would be enough preparation to perform oral surgery?

Don't let these potentially devastating consequences deter

you, though. The trick to faking it at work is to be as consistent as possible and stick to your bit no matter what. If you said you went to Yale, punch a Harvard grad in the face every once in a while. If you haven't been doing any work because a fictitious palsy has turned your limbs against you, throw an occasional cup of coffee on your boss. He won't mind; you're a hero just for showing up every day in the face of such adversity. Plus, he probably went to Harvard. Stupid Harvardite, walking around like he owns the place.

Unless you're a drug dealer or video-store clerk, you'll have to do something responsible with all the money you've been undeservedly earning, so you're going to have to learn to fake your way through the financial world, too. While stuffing all of your cash in a stocking and putting it under your mattress worked with your middle-school allowance, your biweekly paycheck is a bit too large to fit into a single three-stripe tube sock. Also, you should wash the hosiery every once in a while; most businesses won't accept dollar bills that smell like foot sweat. Instead, you'll have to figure out what kind of account to get at a bank, and probably hire an investment advisor to help make sure you get the most out of your hardly earned cash. Sure, you could do it yourself, but nobody is going to believe that that handful of Chuck E. Cheese prize tickets is an investment or that dropping a quarter on Skee-Ball is technically "playing the markets."

The stakes are high in financial faking it, too. If your lack of knowledge enables your broker to sell you crummy stocks or trick you into going double or nothing on that game of three-card monte, you can end up broke or, worse, in a Dickensian workhouse until you pay off your debts. (Yes, we're assuming whoever you owe money has a time machine and can send you to a Victorian debtors prison. The lesson here, as always, is to never shoot dice with a brilliant, eccentric physicist.) However, if you can effectively fake your way through your professional and financial lives, you will look rich, industrious, and successful, all while secretly taking naps in the bathroom during the workday. If anybody asks, you snore when you go.

Interview Skills

If your job doesn't involve mowing lawns or playing the lotto, odds are you'll have to pass through an interview phase to get hired. If you've already landed an interview, then your potential future employers are already impressed by your résumé. Congratulations. Now they're just checking to see if you are a good person.

Do your research and learn as much as you can about the company. If it's a very professional place to work, then they're going to want a professional to work there, so wear a suit. If it's an off-beat, fun kind of place that would be put off by a suit, then dress more casually. There's no rule on what type of clothes to wear, you just have to dress appropriately to the company culture. Although you should never wear a Hard Rock Cafe–Kansas City T-shirt to any interview, even if you're interviewing to be the manager of the Hard Rock Cafe in Kansas City.

You will often hear that the best approach in interviews is to just be yourself, but unless you are a genuinely charismatic guy, that's a horrible idea. You will probably need to be somebody else. This character that you are going to play is a guy who lands jobs. He is courteous, intelligent, and very coherent.

But you don't have to take yourself too seriously. This is basically a personality test. They're probably interviewing dozens of people and every one will try to act as rigidly professional as possible. If you're the one with a sense of humor, then that will stand out. Here are some lines to score points:

> "My biggest weakness? Probably that I'm too motivated. Also, I tend to steal staplers. So I apologize for that in advance. Say, is that a Swingline?"
>
> "No, no. Thank *you*. I'm sort of an interview fanatic. This is my twelfth today."
>
> "I'll tell you what I led: a whole fucking platoon in 'Nam. Don't tell me there's no way I was old enough to serve in the Vietnam War. I was old enough to die for my country."
>
> "I don't have a weakness. Seriously, take this gun and try to shoot me in the face. It will bounce right off. At least for your sake, I hope it will; it's just a theory I've been toying with."

Remember, you have to stand out and make an impression. Otherwise later that week they'll gloss over your résumé and ask one another, "Who was this guy? I think his name was Garbage Head." Then they'll crumple your résumé into a little ball and throw it into a wastepaper basket, while laughing maniacally. And if they miss the shot, somebody will walk over, pick up your crumpled résumé and slam it into that same wastepaper basket. You don't think they became such a powerful company without knowing how to make an offensive rebound, did you?

Padding Your Résumé

Your résumé is the first thing a potential employer reads about you. If you want to make sure it's not the last, you're going to need to embellish a little. Nobody wants to hire a liar—unless they're running a law firm—so when bending the truth, make sure it doesn't break.

What You Can Lie About

There are certain résumé items that are relatively unverifiable; you can feel free to lie about these. If you're still using your GPA, go ahead and bump it up a point or two or five. As long as it stays relatively believable, in the 3.5 range, no employer is going to call your school to check anything. And if they do, then tell them that you quit. "I didn't know I applied for a job working for Big Brother!" Also feel free to lie about your address, but it's going to be hard to get your paycheck that way.

What You Can Embellish

It's okay to enhance any responsibilities you had in prior jobs. Were you an intern at Sony Records over the summer, or were you an executive assistant? Did you sit at a corner computer and chat all day long, or were you in charge of technical operations and intracommunication? Did you get fired because you were caught masturbating in the break room or did you quit in solidarity with the unjust firing of a minority? Job titles and descriptions are inherently arbitrary, so all "embellishing" can be considered as simply "being optimistic."

What You Can't Lie About

It's going to be uncomfortable when your potential future employer mentions that his daughter also works for the Yale newspaper and has never heard of you. Or that the nonprofit organization you started was actually founded in 1881. By Clara Barton. While it's okay to lie about what you did at university or in your previous job, it's not a good idea to completely make up these universities and jobs, though you are very courageous for saying that you founded the Red Cross during your junior year at Cambridge.

Handshake Rules

You never get a second chance to make a first impression, at least until your mind-erasure ray is finally complete. So if your faking is going to work in a business setting, you need to make sure that your first impression is one of authority and confidence. It all starts with a good firm handshake. Yes, it's a cliché, but it's true. Nothing is as disgusting as a limp handshaker, and bosses will notice this shortcoming. So put some muscle into it.

- Squeeze hard, but not too hard. You're not trying to break the person's hand into a worthless sack of flesh and crushed bone, but you also don't want to throw out a limp, clammy appendage that will make them immediately discount your value as a human being.

- Look the person directly in the eye when shaking his or her hand. A firm handshake without eye contact is like an HJ without lubricant. Painful, unfulfilling, and reminiscent of the tenth grade.

- Don't hold it too long! The other person will think you're starved for human contact, and you don't want to seem needy. At least not at first. Later on your telling stories about how your mom didn't hug you will suffice for that.

Professional E-mailing

Most people of our generation grew up using e-mail as a social tool, not a professional one. For this reason, they often have a hard time finding their footing when using e-mail on the job. Just as calling your boss "Dude" on the phone is inappropriate, you should make sure that your professional e-mails have an appropriate tone.

"Sup muthafuckaaaaa. Nah, jaykay. I'll get to that memo later. Lata Sk8a:)"

This would be a fine e-mail to send to a personal friend who also happens to be a memo and skateboarding enthusiast. On the other hand, it will make a poor impression on the president of your company. How can you make sure the e-mails you're sending are suitably professional?

- Put in proper punctuation and capitalization. Unless you're sending it from a mobile device, you should really capitalize your own name, etc. Tough shit for you, ghost of e. e. cummings!

- No emoticons. We don't care how coyly flirtatious you were being there; your boss doesn't want to see the 8-). You're proud of your new glasses, yes, but you've also got a job to do.

- That may be a HILARIOUS forward your uncle Dave sent you, but keep it to yourself. Your boss has already heard the one about the blonde and the surgeon, so just let it go.

- Put one of those little messages on all your outgoing mail that says this communication is confidential and belongs to your company. Nobody really knows what these things mean, but they sure look important.

Takeaway point: Use common sense when sending out e-mails. If you find yourself questioning whether you should send something or not, you probably shouldn't. And resist the urge to "reply all" at all costs. Only Mailer-Daemon can save you now, and he doesn't give a crap about your career.

Milking Your Expense Account

If you work at a company with more than two employees ("Sorry, Dad, I'm not going to be your CEO. Besides nobody wants to buy your Garbage Pail Kids anymore. I don't care how many mint condition Louise Squeezes you have!"), odds are there will be a company expense account. Companies allot a portion of their budget to pay for certain business-related expenses. The challenge for you is to get some meals and other personal expenses considered "business-related." But this is harder than just throwing a McDonald's receipt at the accountant and yelling, "McSpense it. With cheese."

If you're looking to get a free meal, you're going to have to make it look like a business lunch. Tell your bosses that you need to ask an expert for his opinion on a project you're working on and that you've set up a lunch meeting. Then go out and meet a friend of yours for steaks. Make sure to keep the receipt. When you come back, tell your bosses that your meeting mate was mighty helpful, but he ate like a pig. "He had two steaks, so I just had mashed potatoes. Thanks again!"

If you want to use your expense account to score something free for your house, you're going to have to convince the bosses that you need it for your office. "You know, it's mighty hard to concentrate in here without a couch." Then when you go to purchase it, ask the boys down at the couch depot if you can get a buy-one-get-one-free deal if you promise to pay three times the ticket price. They'll be confused but will obviously agree, and you'll have spent $3,000 on two $1,000 couches—one for the office, the other for your home. When you give your boss the receipt, tell him, "They had one cheaper, but . . . I think we're better than that." He'll agree and you'll recline. Everybody wins. Except for your boss. He loses.

QUICK TIP: Expense that dinner with the prostitute. Technically, it's a business meeting for at least one of you.

When your company is paying for meals, standard gluttonous acts such as eating two steaks at once become common practice.

Giving Presentations

Public speaking is always intimidating, in almost every situation. But when you have to give a presentation in front of your coworkers and bosses then it becomes practically impossible. Don't feel bad, very few people are confident enough to stand in front of a group of coworkers and comfortably give a presentation. It's difficult to sound calm and intelligent at the same time, especially when you're nervous and stupid. If only you knew of a way to relax and become less inhibited. Fortunately, you do.

Before a big presentation, regardless of time of day, go to the bathroom and take a shot or two or three of any hard alcohol you have. Then wash it down with some orange juice or coffee, so nobody smells it on your breath. Suddenly you'll feel more at ease and calm, yet still sober enough to give your presentation. Does this make you an alcoholic? Probably, but an alcoholic with a raise! Now you can afford better booze!

Getting tipsy before giving a presentation will alleviate any performance anxiety you may have. Though drinking during the presentation (shown above) is not recommended.

Office Romances

Nothing says "technically, it's only frowned upon" quite like an office romance. The rules regarding office romances vary from workplace to workplace, but generally it's difficult to prevent employees from dating each other. This vaguely defined taboo should end up being advantageous to you because it thins out the rest of the competition for the heart of the special beauty in the cubicle next door.

The key to starting an office romance is to be so subtle in your flirting that your possibly unwanted attempts will never hold up in court as sexual harassment. Also, make sure your small talk leads to more conversations in the future. Here are some examples:

- "Hey, pick a number between one and ten. I bet you I'll get it in seven guesses."

- "Would you rather have to eat a pint of ice cream every day for the rest of your life, or never be able to eat ice cream ever again? Don't answer now, I'll be back later so you can think about it."

- "Hey. I brought you a Creamsaver. They're delicious."

Whatever you do, never display any signs of physical affection. Thumb wrestling, though playful, will look desperate and weird. The ultimate office romance faux pas is the massage; you might as well tape a sign to your shirt that says, "I plan on masturbating to this human contact later because I'm just that creepy."

While the dead-end nature of your job can create a crushing existential void in your soul, it actually works to your advantage when sowing the seeds of romance. You don't have to be aggressive because you're going to keep seeing the person at work indefinitely. Take it slow, and things will blossom into a beautiful flower of fucking on a copy machine.

Once the relationship turns romantic, it's even more important to be discreet. If office workers love one thing more than chocolate cake, it's gossip. In fact, if they had a chocolate cake with icing that read, "Michael and Sarah are dating!" they'd die happy. Rumors will start about any pair of opposite-sex coworkers who are talking, so try not to arrive at the office at the same time or speak to each other civilly.

In fact, open hostility toward your partner may be the best way to handle things to throw your nosy coworkers off the trail. If one of you is the boss, fire the other one. If not, openly lobby to have him or her fired, perhaps by forwarding the contents of personal e-mails making fun of the boss's toupee/wig to the entire office.

There are very few situations in which it's acceptable to hit a woman, but this is one of them. Should the rumor mill start to get out of hand, walk up to her desk and smack her with an open palm while yelling, "You stupid cunt. I can't BELIEVE you lost that account." Don't worry; she'll understand. Nobody else in the office will, though, and you can secretly meet in the break room to kiss each other's booboos and drink that crummy hot chocolate from the vending machine.

Talking Like You've Got an MBA

In the business world, everyone aspires to attending a top-flight university to get his MBA (Master of Business Administration), a degree that will enable earning thousands of extra dollars a year. However, it's a pretty well-known fact that students don't really learn anything useful while working toward their MBAs. Instead, they have their common sense reinforced, attend numerous happy hours sponsored by large corporations, pay for expensive haircuts, and, most important, memorize meaningless jargon. You can always pick out an MBA in a meeting; she's the one talking about synergizing the value chain. At first, you'll be intimidated by these big words. Then you'll realize they're absolutely inane and utterly meaningless. Instead of spending over a hundred grand on a Kellogg MBA, just learn these stupid buzzwords and ride the jargon rocket to the top of the corporate ladder.

Best practices—Because "the best way of doing something" doesn't sound technical enough.

Core competencies—What a company is good at doing. "Strengths" really doesn't sound like something you'd pay some idiot $130,000 a year to know about.

Deliverable—Something tangible you can turn in at the end of an assignment or project. Remember college? You didn't turn in homework; you created deliverables.

Incentivize—To offer someone a tangible reason to do something. And you thought "incentive" couldn't be turned into a verb!

Low-Hanging Fruit—An easy opportunity that will likely be gobbled up by competitors quickly. Think of a dwarf trying to get a peach off of a tree.

Mission-Critical—MBAs like to sound like astronauts from the 1970s. Bascially, this means that something is crucial to the success of a project.

Online—In the MBA sense, this means that a venture or

project has been functionally integrated into the rest of the organization.

Paradigm—Possibly the worst MBA word of them all. Basically, an analytic framework through which a problem is viewed. When paradigms "shift," it means the prevailing thinking on a subject has changed.

Rollout—Process of introducing a new product to the market. Like a "launch," but more jargony.

Supply Chain—Links through which the individual parts of a product are delivered to its final manufacturer and then into the hands of consumers.

SWOT—Analysis of a business or venture on the basis of its strengths, weaknesses, opportunities, and threats. This basically codifies the way any rational person would look at any decision.

Synergy—Another MBA favorite, this one describes the phenomenon of two things coming together and being better than the sum of their parts. Sex is the best, although not the only, example.

Value Added—This a great useless term for anything that makes an existing product or service better. *Make better-er* was deemed too much of "not really a word" to be used in its stead.

QUICK TIP: Make sure you specify that you want to be paid in cash for your commodities trading; there's no way you're fitting a thousand pork bellies in a studio apartment.

Explaining to Your Boss That You Haven't Done Any Work

The key to doing nothing at your job is to always preface it with one hour of hard work. In one hour you can probably get an entire day's worth of work done. If your boss notices you haven't done anything in seven hours, just show him what you worked on and tell him that he doesn't want a rush job on something this important. As long as you have something tangible to show for your previous efforts, he won't think you're lazy, just slow. He'll understand, and you can go back to playing online poker. Don't let anyone tell you that trying to draw to an inside straight on the river isn't work, baby. They don't understand the highs and lows!

If doing an hour's worth of work is even too much for you, you can always tell the boss that he caught you in a moment of contemplation. "Sorry, I'm just thinking exactly how I need to attack this. I need to organize my thoughts before I put them on paper." If he tells you that doesn't make sense because you're working at a Baskin-Robbins and there are no papers involved in scooping ice cream, he's got a good point. Feel free to let him fire you; you need a better job anyway. Take some Jamoca Almond Fudge for the road, and start sending out your cover letter again.

QUICK TIP: If you are feeling under the weather and can't afford another sick day at work, Miss Manners says the polite thing to do is call in a bomb threat.

Getting Fired with Class

So you lost that big account by showing up visibly drunk for an 11:00 A.M. meeting. Or you spent every morning for the past month perfecting your homemade napalm recipe. There are a million little insignificant things you can do to lose your job, and eventually you're going to do one of them. You'll get called into an empty conference room, and your boss or someone from human resources will explain the situation to you. Security will probably show up shortly, so you're faced with a quick decision. You could try to make a huge dramatic scene here, but it probably won't work. Here's how these episodes usually play out:

Your Boss: "You're fired, You."
You: "You can't fire me! I quit!"
Your Boss: "Um, you can't quit. I already fired you."
You: "I see . . ."

Instead, you should be as contrite as possible. Apologize to your boss for letting him down, explain that you've enjoyed working there, and that you understand it's your own fault. You are not here to burn any bridges . . . yet.

Later that night, however, when your boss takes his expensive sports car over the bridge to go home, set it ablaze with that homemade napalm you've been tinkering with. As his car sinks to the river bottom you better hope to death he knows the rule about lowering his windows and swimming out through them. "I just wanted to scare him a little" isn't a legal excuse. Now you have no job and you're in jail. On the plus side, you look fabulous in orange.

Most people with jobs cannot afford jail time. However, if you plan on getting fired, feel free to be a little creative.

Charitable Donations—Look Generous!

You know how PBS gives you a totebag when you make a donation to your local station? It's not because they think you're going to tote things all over the place in a poor-quality canvas carrying sack, and it's not because they just wanted to give you a gift. That tote bag is a conspicuous sign that, hey, you gave money to PBS. Look everyone, this magnanimous bastard peeled a twenty-five-dollar check off during that telethon like it meant nothing to him!

The point is, if you're going to give to charity, you might as well flaunt it. Everyone who's used a tote bag or sipped from an NPR coffee mug has figured out a subtle way to show off the fact that he's got enough money that he can piss some of it away by donating to some crummy charity run by those weird kids from college. You think that guy flaunting his United Negro College Fund umbrella is actually trying to stay dry? It's a sunny day in August for crying out loud!

It's easier than it sounds. Just find a charity that's taking donations, and make a small one, probably something like twenty-five bucks. (It's a tax deduction, so it won't even end up costing that much.) Make sure you're going to get some sort of

Collecting charity giveaways is a great way to seem altruistic regardless of how many orphans you mistreat on a daily basis.

tangible item in return. Try not to seem so transparent when donating, though. "Got anything with one of them starving Africans right on the T-shirt?" "In a large?" "No, the shirt, not the starving African." Then, when you get it, leave it somewhere obvious in your apartment and don't mention it. When guests come over, they'll think, "Wow, this guy's really generous." In economics, this is known as conspicuous consumption; in Sunday school, it's called doing the right thing for the wrong reason.

Faking Sleeper Companies

The only portfolio you own is an old Lisa Frank Trapper Keeper, but somehow you've been pulled into a conversation about stock picks. Words like *market cap, price-to-earnings ratio,* and *broker* are probably being bandied about, and you have no idea what's going on. Don't get in over your head here. Instead of trying to hang with the conversation, start talking about sleeper stocks.

Don't worry that you don't know any actual sleeper companies. Between the New York Stock Exchange and the NASDAQ, there are over six thousand companies. No one knows them all. String together words that sound like reasonable names for a tech company. "I think Unified Synergies is trading a little low right now and could really come on strong next quarter." There's no company called Unified Synergies, but no one there will know it. Same with Compucyberdyne, Advanced Network Systems Solutions Dot Net, and, to a lesser extent, Paul's Fish 'n' Sorbet, Inc.

"Oh, I haven't heard of them, what do they do?" Good question. It's time to get more vague. Your fictional company can specialize in anything from "supply-chain consulting" to "information systems" to even "human capital management." These are all dead-end, boring answers that require no further elaboration.

Without reading a single issue of *The Wall Street Journal,* you will hold everyone in awe of your mastery of the little nuances of the markets, the hard-to-find diamonds in the rough, whether or not they exist. Now, hope they don't immediately call their brokers and find out there's no company on the NAS-DAQ called Robotics for Tomorrows.

Seeming Affluent

While very few people have the financial security to purchase many expensive items, most people have the money to purchase at least one. If you want to seem richer than you actually are, you need to sacrifice the quality of many possessions in order to obtain a few very noticeably luxurious ones.

For example, if you only have $1,000 to spend on your living room, instead of buying an average couch, an average coffee table, an average lamp, and an average TV, you can buy a $1,000 plasma TV and get the rest of your furniture for nearly nothing on Craigslist or on the street. The large fancy TV, coupled with the "rustic-looking" furniture, makes you out to be some eccentric millionaire who prefers humble furniture over being the first owner of his sofa. Just make sure you formulate some lie about how this was a conscious artistic decision rather

Spending most of your disposable income on one noticeable item can make any hobo seem like a millionaire.

than one mandated by your budget. "You know, I just wanted to try to recapture part of the decorative arts sensibility of my childhood; it's a nostalgia thing, I guess."

The same can go for your clothes. Spend the most money on clothing you'll have to wear the most, and for the other stuff, you can get it for dirt cheap. A $1,000 suit can go a long way, but if you never wear a suit, spend your money on something else—perhaps a winter coat. If most of the time that coat will cover up the rest of your clothes, splurge on that and skimp on the rest. The only difference between seeming rich and being rich is that rich people have a closet full of expensive clothing at home and you may not even have a home—but nobody is going to be seeing those clothes anyway.

Takeaway point: You don't have the funds to improve every facet of your life. Instead, choose one conspicuous item that would mean the most to you, and splurge on that. The rest of your less expensive items can be brushed underneath the metaphorical bed that is your life, never to see the light of day.

Robbing a Bank

Are you broke the night before a big expensive dinner date? Yeah, we've been known to bet on the outcomes of shows on the History Channel, too. Don't you think you would have heard about it if the Germans had won World War II, though? Nevertheless, you need money—and lots of it. There's no honest way to get this cash, so you're going to have to rob a bank. Now, we know what you're thinking: "I can't rob a bank; that's a crime." Quit being a pussy. Do you want to have money or not? Well, banks are like money factories. You basically just have to walk in and take all of the sweet cabbage, son.

The most important part of bank robbery is to talk like a character from a heist movie from the 1930s. This vocal tic will help you seem more authentic. Say that you're "knocking the bank over," and whenever you say anything, add "See?" to the end of the sentence. This sounds supertough. Trust us. After you've learned to talk in this voice for a few minutes at a time, purchase a bandana and sunglasses. These will constitute your disguise when you knock over the joint, see? Next, pick a firearm (we suggest a Tommy gun), run into the bank, yelling something intimidating. "Give me the money and nobody gets hurt!!!!" is an oldie but a goodie. Some warning shots into the

Robbing a bank may seem like easy money, but only if you don't get caught. Make sure to escape police and don't get cocky. Your next heist may be your last.

air will ensure nobody tries to be a hero. Take the money and run. The best thing is that technically it's not stealing if you force somebody to give you the money at gunpoint.*

Getting Your Cable Bill Reduced

Your cable company is evil, and it is the enemy of your bank account. There's no two ways about it. They make you wait for

---

*Completely untrue.

hours every time you want to get a home repair, they overcharge you, and the on-demand softcore rarely has ribald titles like *Good Will Cunting.* However, you can turn the tables on them with a quick bill reduction.

Remember when you signed up for cable they put you on some sort of special rate for six months? Then after the six months, your bill doubled. Well, at most cable companies, you can get the special rate back with a phone call. Here's what you do:

1. Call the customer service number on your bill. Explain that your service has simply gotten too expensive for you, and you think you might have to cut it off. Now, to the cable company, this sounds catastrophic. The marginal cost of having another subscriber is so low that they're effectively losing nothing but profit when you stop sending them a check every month. Tell them you think you can survive without their stupid Lifetime original movies. Little do they know you actually can't. Shannen Doherty–made-for-TV movies are like insulin to you.

2. They'll probably refer you to their retention line, which is usually staffed by cheery people whose job it is to retain customers. Simply explain again, being very polite and remembering your "ma'am," "sir," and "thank yous." Make it sound like you are breaking up with them. "Listen, it's not you, it's E!"

3. At some point, they'll offer you some sort of retention

special. This is effectively the same rate you were paying as your sign-up special, and you'll save thirty or forty bucks a month. Thank them effusively. "I promise I won't let you down. I'll be the best subscriber you'll ever have. Just wait and see!" and when this special runs out in six months, simply call back.

4. Invest the savings in roulette: Purchase your own cable company with your winnings. We recommend Time Warner.

Handling Your Change

Every time you make a purchase with cash, you get a handful of change back. It seems frivolous to throw that ninety-seven cents away, but the constant jangling in your pocket gets annoying. You could dump it all in a drawer, or you could really make it work for you. Here's how:

- Get a large glass bowl, bottle, or vase and put it somewhere prominent in your home. Place a brochure next to the bowl that features sad-looking children. You can get these at mostly any sad-looking-children-brochure outlet. Every day, dump your change in the bowl.

- As it begins to fill with change, people will begin asking what the deal with this change bucket is. Tell them, "Oh, I just put my change in there, and whenever it gets full, I cash it in and give it to a different charity. It's just a little thing I do to try to help."

- When the jar actually fills up, take it to a Coinstar, then use the money to buy a duffel bag full of 3 Musketeers bars. Suckers!

QUICK TIP: If you're trying to impress a religious lady, tell her you donate 10 percent of your salary to the church. When she asks which one, tell her you only have one salary and that you don't understand her question. Then change the subject.

The Quick $100

There will come a time where you will need a quick $100. Basketball tickets, fancy dinner, birthday present, yes, literally anything can cost you $100. Unfortunately that's $100 more than what is currently in your bank account. Here are some quick ways to earn that Benjamin Franklin rookie card:

eBay

Pros: Not only are you making money, but you are opening up spaces in your garage that were otherwise occupied by Atari games collecting dust since 1981.

Cons: It may take a while before the auction finally closes and you get paid. This one requires some planning ahead.

Tips: Make sure to start the auction during a workday, as last-minute bidding may up the final sales price. If an auction ends at 4:00 A.M., nobody is going to bid it up at the last minute.

Donating Plasma

Pros: Plasma donations don't remove red blood cells and platelets from your circulatory system, meaning you can safely donate twice a week.

Cons: Needles. If you hate getting blood drawn, then it may not be worth the money.

Tips: Donating plasma is more lucrative than donating blood, so do a simple Google search for plasma donation centers in your city, or just call up a hospital and ask them. And try not to be rude; they're less likely to refer you if you yell at them, "Where the plasma money at!? Give it here!"

Craigslist Odd Jobs

Pros: If you have nothing better to do, helping somebody move or transcribing audio to text pays better than you think.

Cons: You may have something better to do.

Tips: Search the community section of your city's Craigslist page, and see what people are desperate for. Some people will pay for a cat sitter, other people just need a van for the day. For most people this is a last resort, so you can use that as leverage when negotiating.

Mugging

Pros: Most people are too young to die. They'll do anything to stay alive.

Cons: You may go to jail and posting bail will probably cost you more than $100.

Tips: Legally, we can't give you proper mugging tips. However, a Butterfinger bar in your pocket looks just like a gun.

Most of your important organs come in pairs, whereas only one is necessary to live. You do the math.

QUICK TIP: No amount of accessorizing is going to make the canvas vest you have to wear for work look dignified. Also, clean up on aisle three.

Jobs That Pay Well While Requiring No Education

So you can scrap together a couple hundred bucks every now and then, but odds are you're more concerned about getting a real job. However, you dropped out of college or, even worse, spent four years in there getting an English degree. Now, instead of being broke, you're hundreds of thousands of dollars in debt. (Did you steal this book or get it as a gift?)

Not all hope is lost, though, because you don't need a college degree to land a high-paying job. Some lines of profession don't even trust colleges and spend a couple months or years training you to do their job. Sounds annoying right? Well, it is. That's why they pay the people who actually do complete the training a good amount of money. Here are some great examples, and just think, by this time tomorrow you could be reading this book in *new* boxers.

Air Traffic Controller—Do you like wearing noise-cancelling headphones? Well, then this is the profession for you! After a rigorous training program that can last as little as six months, you can become an air traffic controller. This is one of the highest paying jobs in America because the work shifts are considered extremely stressful. But for a salary of over $100,000 a year, you can budget at least $100 for really powerful stress balls.

Bartender—You know when you go to a bar you leave a dollar on the counter after every drink you get? Well, other people do that, too. Sometimes even two or three dollars. Multiply that by the amount of people you see in the bar and you've got yourself a lot of money. Bartenders don't get paid much hourly, but if you're at a relatively popular place, you can make a great deal of money in tips. (We believe the scientific term is "a shit load.") Bartending schools aren't so difficult to get into and not very expensive. Besides, free booze means you're also cutting your most costly expense. Now, if you could also just get that job at the cereal factory, you'd be set.

Real Estate Broker—You know what separates you from people who can sell houses? Just a real estate license. You haven't studied for a test in years, so hopefully you have lots of brain cells in reserve. Take some time and try to pass a real estate license exam. Agents work on commission, but luckily for you houses are expensive. That's probably why your landlord is so pissed you haven't paid rent in three months.

Professional Roulette Player—You don't need a degree to be lucky. The great thing about roulette is that over time, you simply cannot lose. Especially when you know the extra lucky numbers: 1, 9, 23, 25, 34, 36! Now the only question is, what are you going to do with your first million bucks? Our suggestion: Let it ride on third twelve, it's due for a hit!

CHAPTER 4

The Sporting Life

It's very difficult to fake athletic ability, which is probably why sports teams spend so much time practicing. You can talk all you like about what a great basketball or football player you were in high school, but the minute someone calls you out, you'll end up revealing that your "killer fastball" is thrown underhand and probably couldn't kill a baby. Unless it lands square on the soft spot, though with your aim that's highly unlikely. Successfully faking it at the gym or on the playing field requires a clever blend of saying the right things, avoiding actual competition, and carefully covering your tracks.

No one knows why sports and athletic competition are valued so highly by our society, but they always have been. Thus, if you are bad at basketball, you're not just unathletic. You're a disgrace. You're a pussy. You're barely even a man. Yes, no matter how much money you make, how many times you've received tenure at Harvard, or how many women you've slept with, your value to society is dictated by how well you can perform at a game favored by unemployed teenagers. Since you're probably a little late for the hey-let's-get-good-at-sports! boat, your only choice is to cheat, fake, and ladder-assist dunk your way to glory.

Obviously, though, you'll get a free pass from all of this judgment if you have some sort of disability, so you might want to consider feigning a serious injury that would forever prevent you from taking part in sports. A fragile ACL is nice, but being a full-on paraplegic can get you a lifetime exemption from office softball and a seat in the big bathroom stall. Plus, imagine how good you'll be at wheelchair basketball when you can occasionally stand up and get a running start for your layups. Other acceptable, if more subtle, excuses include arthritis, migraines, and the ever popular "You know my mom got murdered by a basketball . . . it's too soon for me to even touch one."

Even if you never set foot on the playing field, chances are your physical prowess or lack thereof will eventually be put on display at the gym. In terms of completely avoidable sources of stress that people inject into their lives, going to the gym ranks right behind trying heroin for the first time. You start going because you want to tone up your frame and maybe meet some girls. You then quickly realize that you're not going to get twenty-inch biceps by doing a hundred pushups a week, no matter how loudly you grunt as you do them, and girls aren't really approachable when sweating profusely on an elliptical with iPod headphones planted firmly in their ears. The easiest way to fake your way out of an embarrassing gym situation is to just never go to the gym. If someone asks you how often you go to the gym say, "Not very often. I got a membership to one across town, but I never go." Ninety percent of people are in this situation, so your story will check out, and nobody will look for you to have perfect abs. If you simply must go to the gym, you can always try to get there before the daily rush, then leave as everyone shows up. People will think you've been throwing up some serious weight for hours, when really you've just been walking on a treadmill and watching *ALF* reruns. They'll think you're sweating out of your eyes, but you're actually crying because you realize in one episode, ALF has eaten more cats than you will in your entire life.

For more specific tips about football, look for this book's sequel, *Faking It: Punts and Field Goals,* due out next year.

Getting Out of Playing Sports

Much like it's better to keep one's mouth shut and be thought a fool than open it and remove all doubt, it's better to stay on the sidelines of a game like a wuss than have everyone find out you throw and run like a prepubescent girl. Try some of these tactics to avoid embarrassing yourself:

- Cramp up when you're warming up. Cramps are great because they're completely debilitating but have no visible symptoms and won't linger into the next day. Yes, you can feign a broken arm, but everyone's going to expect to see you in a cast the next day. They bought a special marker set and everything so they could sign it!

- Cite a fictitious, previously sustained injury. Did you tear your ACL playing football in high school? Well, you did now, and you can't play an impromptu pickup game without your knee brace. Ultimate Frisbee? Sounds fun, but you have tennis elbow. Tell the gang, "It's more serious than it sounds," then whip out the towel, place it on the floor, and read *Archie Comics*. "I'll be in Riverdale if you need me!"

- Claim you don't have the right equipment. These jokers want you to play soccer without cleats? Yeah, right—if you want your ankles broken, you'll have someone hit them with a hammer.

- It's common knowledge that anybody with asthma can't do much of anything active. Pick up a used inhaler from the children's hospital and carry it around. If anybody proposes anything athletic, wave it around like a police badge of laziness. Tell them to run along now or you'll start hyperventilating.

- Mystery illness is the greatest excuse since sliced dog eating my homework. Sports gatherings are filled with know-it-all doctor types who have seen every injury in the book. Throw them for a loop by describing conflicting symptoms of all kinds. "Jesus, I feel really light-headed and tense right now. I dunno, it's weird. My ankle and brain are hurting." This usually scares your sports mates into saying, "Maybe you should just sit down and get some water." Nobody wants to see somebody die; it ruins any pickup game.

- If the game is softball or baseball, take the bat and brutally beat half of your fellow athletes. Look the others dead in the eyes and say, "I don't feel like I have my swing back. I'll sit this one out." Hop on your motorcycle and roar out of town, blood spattered on your riding chaps, never to be seen again.

Cramps are a great excuse to pass on sporting events as long as you don't mind ice packs.

How to Cheat at Scrabble

If you're in dire need of a letter, put any tile you have on the board facedown and people will assume it is a blank. This will work as long as people don't realize there are only two blank tiles in the whole game and both of them are already in play. Also, a little Sharpie, some creativity, and sleight of hand will turn any J into a Q, though this rarely helps.

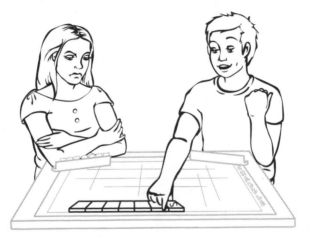

Placing the tiles on the board blank side up is a great way to cheat at Scrabble, but don't use it too liberally. Three to four blanks every turn should suffice.

Ten-Minute Workouts

No one is going to mistake you for being in the middle of an anabolic steroids cycle if you're on a ten-minute-a-day exercise regimen, but in a time crunch, on vacation, or before a date, a quick session is better than nothing. You'd be surprised

at how comprehensive a workout you can get with ten minutes of high-intensity exercise. The following doesn't even require dumbbells or a gym, so you're fresh out of excuses,
bagel face.

Cardio

Meet the jump rope, your new best friend and one of myriad
reasons why boxers can beat the piss out of you. Jumping
rope is cheap, less tedious than running, and works your
heart, shoulders, and calves. A brisk three-minute warmup
followed by five one-minute sprints (with a thirty-second rest
after each one) and you'll be sucking wind in no time. Please
avoid hiring two African American nine-year-olds to double-
Dutch you. We don't care how much yellow Cinderella was

Jumping rope is a great way to get a quick cardio workout, but
you should learn to do it alone rather than relying on the aid of
neighborhood schoolgirls.

dressed in, she just couldn't have wanted to meet her fella that much!

Strength

An elastic resistance band (available at Target or at most athletic stores) is one of the most cost-effective training tools out there. You can work the same muscle groups (at the same intensity) as you can with dumbbells, while saving yourself the trouble of working out in the same room as a bunch of grunting meatsticks. The premise behind the elastic band is simple—the less slack you give it, the more resistance it gives, and the harder your muscles work. There are thousands of different exercises you can perform with a band, but if you only have ten minutes, stick with the beach muscles: arms, chest, and shoulders.

- Bicep Curls: Stand on the band (the wider, the more tension produced), knees slightly bent, and grip each end of the band. With palms facing out, bring band toward shoulder and then back down. Two sets, eight–twelve reps each. Flex in front of the mirror for five minutes afterward, tapping your biceps, convincing yourself that they are much bigger than you thought they were.

- Tricep Pushdown: Wrap band around something that will keep it in place (doorknob, pole, tree, etc.), and grip each end of the band. With your back straight and your elbows in, push each end of the band down until your elbow forms a ninety-degree angle with the ground.

Slowly release. Two sets, eight–twelve reps each. Straighten your arms trying to feel the soreness of your triceps already. Tell yourself you're going to be needing a bigger shirt soon.

- Chest Press: Wrap band around something that will keep it in place. With one leg staggered forward and knees slightly bent, grip each end of the band. Slowly press arms forward as you bring hands together, return to starting position. Two sets, eight–twelve reps each. Try to make your pecs jiggle and fail. Convince yourself that the pec jiggle is a "gay move," anyway.

- Lateral Raises: Stand with feet shoulder-width apart on top of band and grip each end with hand. Slowly raise your arms out to the side until they are lateral with your shoulders. Return to starting position. Two sets, eight–twelve reps each. Yell at the end of each rep because you're a rabid animal. When your mom comes in because she's rather concerned, tell her to "Get the fuck outta here! God! Don't you ever knock anymore, slut!? Yeah, meatloaf is fine; just get out!"

Look Like You've Been Lifting More

Nobody wants to get off the bench-press machine and have the young lady who was waiting see he was struggling against seventy pounds. Instead, make it look like you were throwing up some serious weight by discreetly moving the pin further down the stack. This way, she'll get on the machine and see

By moving the pin down the stack of weights after finishing your set, the next person to use that machine will think you are a stronger, and therefore better, person.

that you were throwing up a deuce and a half. Sure, your arms would probably look bigger if that were the case, but who knows?

Don't Lift—Spot!

Want to be known as the kind of beefy dude who hangs out in the gym all day, but don't like lifting heavy things? Get a gym membership and a loose-fitting T-shirt, and begin spotting everyone in sight. You'll quickly gain a reputation as that helpful guy who's always at the gym, so you must be pretty cut underneath that extra-large Beefy Tee, right? Nobody will know that your only athletic skill consists of lightly pulling on a bench-press bar with your index fingers, shouting, "Come on, one more. Good."

Arm Wrestling: The Pissing Contest of Choice

Every man will agree that arm wrestling is a great way to determine how strong, and therefore, how awesome, somebody truly is. Unfortunately for you, the most physical activity you've ever done involved a Power Pad and your eight-year-old sister. Fortunately for you, when it comes to arm wrestling there are many ways to fake strength.

While muscle mass is an important factor in arm wrestling, technique is even more crucial. A scrawny loser like yourself may even be able to beat some gym-going hoodlums with the proper form. Here's what you can do:

The Top Roll: When the match starts, creep your hand as high as it can go on your opponent's hand, then try to roll your hand over the top of his. This will cause him great discomfort and allow you to put your full body weight on his arm. As long as he can't curl your entire body weight, this should be enough pressure for you to win. Spit on his chin when you're done and tell him to hit the shower. He smells like cottage cheese.

The Pull-in: As the match begins, pull your opponent's arm close to you and squeeze his hand. This should shock him for just enough time to put your entire body on top of your hand and squish his down to the floor. He should be shocked and in pain so feel free to use the next three seconds to throw your hands up in the air and declare that you are the strongest man alive. Because for this brief moment, according to everybody else, you are.

The Psych-out: Before the match, do some background checks on your opponent. Find out his social security number and credit card information. When the match begins and you two struggle in limbo together, begin spouting out information that will freak him out. "554-29-2921. Your mother's maiden name is Linfield. At age five you lost a cat to AIDS. At age seventeen you lost your girlfriend in a minimall, but later found her, but then lost her later that day to Cancer. Cancer was the boy next

Although these techniques may work against your friend's enemies, don't rush into joining every arm-wrestling tournament this side of Siberia. The best finish you could possibly hope for is third, and the prize for that will probably be some shitty vacation—not worth it.

door." As he cries from full disclosure and begs you to stop, let him know that the only thing that will shut you up is a victory. He'll relent and you can pin him. Then pick his girlfriend up and tongue-kiss her. She's yours now.

Yoga—Don't Underestimate It

You know that hot girl at your gym? The one that makes you wish now, more than ever, that you were a gym towel? The one that causes all the muscle men around her to start their bench press counts at fifty? What these muscle monkeys don't realize is that the fastest way to her incredibly healthy heart isn't through her eyes, it's through her chi. Nothing impresses that hot gym-rat quite like a man doing yoga.

Yoga is a spiritual date-rape drug. By sucking it up and joining that 8:00 A.M. class at your gym, you are giving off the following message: "I'm a sensitive guy who isn't only worried about my physical appearance and how big I get, I'm also concerned about my spiritual well-being. Also, I'm not afraid to embarass myself in front of others or break a little sweat before work. Furthermore, that farting noise I keep emitting during downward dog isn't silly to me, it's a spiritual release. And lastly, I'm extra-bendy in the sack."

Not only is yoga a gold mine for attractive gym-goers, it gives you a chance to be cute and self-deprecating in their presence, and they love that. If you think they're impressed by your biceps and ability to chug protein shakes at an alarming rate, you're mistaken. Also, odds are you will be the only male in there because most guys think yoga is for pussies. Well, if getting phone numbers from cute girls is for pussies, get ready to be the sloppiest, wettest pussy in town!

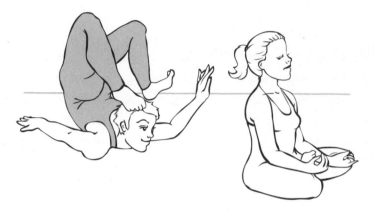

A yoga class is a great venue to meet and inadvertently ogle available, flexible women.

Dunking a Basketball

You may have no athletic ability. You may be devoid of any physical prowess. You may be more uncoordinated than a three-legged elephant. However, there is one maneuver, when performed correctly, that will leave people automatically believing that you are the best sportsman alive.

Dunking a basketball is the ultimate way to fake athletic talent. It instantly transforms any nerd into, at the very least, Clyde Drexler. So instead of spending time learning how to dribble or shoot, just follow these tips and you'll be able to wow anybody in no time.

1. The rim is ten feet high so you're going to need a running start. Begin jogging from about half court, then sprinting at the three-point line.

2. You should take off at around the middle of the key, leaving yourself plenty of space to reach the rim. As you take off, yell, "I'm 'bout to hurt all y'all!"

3. In order to ensure that your dunk isn't a weak one, make sure to get at least your elbow over the front of the rim. It may be tempting to break the backboard, but you're trying to earn some cred, not become an attention whore.

4. Throw it down with maximum force so as to ensure extreme intimidation. As the ball bounces back up off the court, you may want to consider grabbing it and dunking it again. Yes, gravity will allow it if you believe it will.

5. On your way back down to earth, land on both feet and let out a primal scream. Look your defender dead in the eye and point out you were all up in his business, which you should pronounce "biz-nass."

There it is! Pretty easy, huh? And the best part about it is, those idiots don't even know that in actuality, you are a completely unathletic loser with absolutely no speed or vertical leaping ability. See you in the showers, suckers!

QUICK TIP: Keep things fresh by throwing in an occasional reverse, windmill, or three-sixty dunk. If you are going to fake athletic ability, you might as well go all out. For maximum effect, try to toss in that helicopter-tomahawk hybrid with the *whoosh-whoosh-whoosh* noise from the original *NBA Jam*.

You'll want to get at least your elbow above the rim if you plan on really intimidating people, but be careful about hitting your face on the backboard.

Riding a Bike to Work

If you live within five miles from your job, riding your bike to work is incredibly good for your heart, wallet, and social life. The twenty to thirty minutes you ride your bike each way won't seem like a big deal at the time but keep it up and it will help you burn the calories you gain during the day stealing people's birthday cupcakes. Also, the money you are saving on gas will far outweigh the cost of the bike and any legal fees brought upon you when people sue you for stealing their cupcakes. And lastly, riding a bike is usually considered off-beat and hip enough that, when coupled with a new slender you and some extra money, it will persuade that hot girl in human resources to give you a date. Say, dinner at Sizzler then dessert at the local cupcakery? Yup, riding a bike to work has never been sweeter . . .

Faking Your Way Through a Sports Party

Every sports-loving group of friends usually has one member who knows absolutely nothing. However, he is still invited over to watch the big game with everybody else, but only because he likes the company and the seven-layered dip (and more specifically, the cheese layer). If this person is you, you should still know how to act at a sports party, even if you don't know the difference between a 6-4-3 double play and a 3-2-3 double play, moron!

> Don't: Ask who the "red team" is. There's nothing that makes you sound more ignorant about sports than reducing a team to a color. Just wait until one of the teams scores and check to see how the scoreboard changes. Or wait for a close-up and read the names on the front of the jerseys, that's the one that counts.

> Do: Keep your mouth as shut as possible. Most of the time, sports parties are accompanied by conversations about sports. And the only thing you can contribute is "Why do you guys know all this shit? Don't you ever watch anything else?" If you just keep to yourself and enjoy your

cheese layer in silence, nobody will be angry at you. But stop skimming off the top, nobody wants six-layered dip!

Don't: Change the channels during the commercials. Half the fun of sports parties is watching the testosterone-infused commercials and making fun of them. And while most are horrible, there are a couple of sweet ones and if you change the channel to watch *The Pelican Brief* on TBS during time-outs, no one's going to see them. Besides, you can't just watch that movie in five-minute increments—a Grisham movie demands more respect than that.

The ignorant sports type is wise to stay silent at parties and enjoy his true athletic passion: chips with dip.

Do: Try to get into the game. Most non-sports fans can find something exciting about a particular game's story line. Choose a favorite team and become a fan for three hours. Then when they lose, bang your fist on the table, stare up to the ceiling and begin tearing up. Mutter, "It wasn't supposed to end this way. We played too damn hard to lose this game. Fuck!!!!!!!!!!!" Your friends will think they have converted you; little do they know you're just still reeling over the lack of dip.

QUICK TIP: "I only watch it for the commercials" works for the Super Bowl, but nobody's buying it when they catch you watching *Dharma & Greg* reruns.

Faking an Eye Exam

Glasses are for nerds and jerks, so it's important to pass every eye exam you take. Pass it with flying colors, and your handsome face will never be sullied by nerdy frames. Unfortunately, your vision's been failing you in the past few years. Don't worry; just learn the chart ahead of time, and pass with ease.

First Row: E
Second Row: F P
Third Row: T O Z
Fourth Row: L P E D

and so on. Congrats, hawkeye. Oh, one little thing. That hot optometrist's assistant you've been flirting with is a nineteen-year-old boy, and he's more than a little uncomfortable about the whole thing.

Sports-Betting Lingo

It's a tough situation. You don't know anything about sports, but you also don't want to seem like a retard around your new friends when they ask you whether or not they should "Parlay the over with the money line on those four-point dogs."

Since there's no way you plan on gaining an interest in sports after all these years, the next best thing you can do is at least know what the hell they're talking about. That way you'll seem slightly more manly when taking in a day of shopping and a Cirque du Soleil show, while your friends are yelling at the giant TVs at the sports bar.

So here's everything you need to know. Every sporting event has a favorite and an underdog (or "dog" for short). So let's say the Pistons are playing the Celtics, and the Pistons are favored by seven. That's basically like asking, if you take the final score and subtract seven from the Pistons, will they still win? If you think the answer is yes, you bet on them, if not, then you bet on the Celtics.

Question: The Lakers are favored by four over the Trail Blazers, and you bet twenty dollars on them to cover the spread. They win the game 98–95. Did you win your bet?

Answer: If you take away four from the Lakers score, would they still win? The answer is no, and so you lost your bet. Congrats, you could have had a nice buffet brunch with that cash, too. That'll teach you not to gamble with your allowance.

You can also bet on total score, rather than on which team you think will win. That's the over-under. Usually for a basketball game, the over-under is around 200 (about 100 for each team). If you think the game will be low scoring, you'll want to take the under. If you think the game will be high scoring, you should take the over.

Question: The over/under for the Knicks-Bulls game is 193, and you bet fifty dollars on the over. The Knicks won 101–98. Did you win your bet?

Answer: Yes! The total score was 199, which was over Vegas's prediction of 193. You just won fifty dollars! Now go blow that on roulette so that the poor casino makes its money back. Caesar's has to put food on the table, too!

Where Your Sports Gambling Winnings Will Go:

99 percent: Future Sports Gambling Losses
1 percent: Lunch Buffet

Guess What? You're Training to Run a Marathon!

Interesting fact: There is no visible difference between somebody training to run a marathon and somebody who says he's training to run a marathon. Telling people that you are training to run a marathon is easily the most impressive and effortless lie in the history of lying (and it is a very storied history indeed). Marathon training occurs early in the morning before anybody wakes up, and even better, if you live in a large city, half the time people apply for marathons, they don't get accepted to actually run.

So Here Is What You Need to Know

The race is 26.2 miles long.
You have to apply months in advance.
Training takes about twenty-five weeks.
Training consists of five runs a week, with the long one every Sunday. You are supposed to raise your Sunday run by one mile every week.

What You Need to Say

"Yeah, I mostly train at 5:00 or 6:00 A.M. It gets my blood flowing before work."
Reasoning: They will never ask to come along for a day or see you afterward, if you are training at ungodly hours.

"It's bullshit. You spend all this time training and they still won't let you run the race."
Reasoning: Some marathons require you to enroll into a lottery system and they choose runners at random. They won't be choosing you. Tell people you are legally barred from running this race, otherwise you'd be all over it. Perfect.

"Most people don't know this, but total weekly and total monthly mileage is as important as individual runs."

Reasoning: This idea is in chapter one of any marathon book. We just saved you twenty dollars. And now you can convince even real marathon trainers of your intent to run in this unnecessarily long race. (Note: Do not call it "unnecessarily long." In fact, call it "a little short for your liking.")

"Stretching is critical to training, not as much before the run but afterward; it's the most important way to prevent training-ending injury."

If you are going to fake an injury before a marathon, at least have the common sense to dress as if you were planning on racing.

Reasoning: You need to know something about stretching and act like a training-ending injury would be worse than cancer for you right now. "I can run through cancer, but a pulled hammy takes weeks to recover!"

Important note: It's tough to lie about this stuff with a cigarette in your mouth and ketchup stains on your shirt. At least have the common decency to take that ham out of your mouth, you fat slob.

CHAPTER 5

The Handyman

Despite social stereotypes and expectations, most men can't fix anything. If you're extremely rich, this shortcoming isn't a predicament. Lose your TV remote? A quick call to Best Buy can have a new plasma screen on your wall in minutes! Remember, changing batteries is for the poor, so just throw that remote away.

For those of us with normal bank accounts and cigarette lighters instead of flaming hundred dollar bills, these issues can get a bit trickier. You can try taking the rich guy's strategy as your own, but soon your wallet is going to start feeling pretty thin. Instead, you're going to have to bear down and learn how to fix things. That, or you're going to have to learn how to fake your way through it. Luckily, all but a small marginally employed fraction of the population are absolutely horrendous at any sort of handyman work, so you're unlikely to be caught in your web of lies.

At its most basic level, you can fake handiness just by learning the names of every tool. Knowing the difference between a crescent wrench and pliers will get you through the most basic and welcome situation: A friend fixes everything and you just hand him the tools while he works. It's important to know what you're doing here, though, because when he asks for a Phillips head screwdriver, you don't want to yell, "Okay, Phil's head is a little small, but you know he's sensitive about it. Jesus, I don't know why you have to bring it up every few seconds!" Congratulations, three-year-old kids who watch Bob the Builder cartoons would make more knowledgeable repairmen than you would.

You can rationalize your lack of mechanical ability all you like. This is something your dad should have taught you, but he was never home. (No, he wasn't a workaholic—he was in prison for five years.) It's not your fault the damn car broke—why didn't those lazy slobs at the plant build it more carefully? That's union labor for you. However, no amount of complaining is going to fix your problem, so eventually it's going to be time for you to take care of business. Here's where the faking comes in.

At this point, you must seek professional help and guidance for your problem, so instead of trying to fake your way through the fixing process, you have to explain why you can't fix it. In fact, you can fake a pretty comprehensive mechanical knowledge without ever getting your hands dirty if you know exactly what to say at any moment. There is always some conceivable reason that you can't fix something in your home, and it's never "I have no idea what a carburetor is, what it does, or how to spell it." Pay attention to this chapter, and you'll come out fine.

The Magic of Owning a Drill

So you want everyone to think you're some sort of handyman genius even though you have no idea how to use a hammer? Don't worry, the ownership of a single tool can solve most of your problems. Those wanting to seem like an expert despite their complete lack of knowledge need to buy only one thing: a cordless drill. You spend less than a hundred bucks on one of these bad boys, and you can drill a hole in whatever you want. Plus, you can put together prefab bookshelves and tables in mere seconds with a screwdriver bit. This means that everyone will want for you to help with his lame Ikea purchases, and you'll become the "guy who's good with tools." Little did they know that you think a hex wrench has something to do with voodoo.

Easy Things to Fix

You might not be able to fix most things, but the occasional little flourish can trick people into thinking you can. The following items are generally pretty easy to fix:

- Toilet. If it's constantly running, take the lid off the tank and see if the stopper at the bottom is making a seal. If not, mash it down into place with your fingers, and the tank will slowly fill up. If the handle won't make it flush, remove the lid and make sure the little chain that runs down from the handle hasn't gotten disconnected. Occasionally, none of this will work and you'll have to replace the internal workings. Don't get too nervous here; just go to a hardware store and buy the kit. The instructions are completely self-explanatory, and there's no way you can screw them up. If all else fails, throw an M-80 into the bowl and hit the deck. If you can't fix something, you may as well play a timeless prank.

- Jammed lock. Unless you've broken a key off in it, you can usually get a troublesome lock to pop open with a squirt or two of WD-40. In fact, keep WD-40 around at all times. It's great for lubricating metals, and it can remove tape or glue residue as well. You'll look like a genius for spending two bucks on a can. Use it on squeaky hinges, stuck lawn-mower blades, etc. Don't use it to make one of those sweet blowtorches, though; girls haven't been impressed by your ability to roast ants since the ninth grade.

- Nuclear fission reactor. The control rods are jammed in the up position?! We'd tell you how to fix it, but you're probably already dead. Oops!

Excuses for Getting Out of Fixing Things

From toilets to tires, a wide array of items can easily break or flatten and any guy who cannot fix them will be completely and utterly emasculated in front of his friends, lovers, and appliances. So you've got two options: start learning how to fix everything in sight (which sounds like an awful lot of effort), or come up with reasonable, realistic-sounding excuses for why you need to seek professional help. The key is to be vague while still using enough technical terms that it sounds like you know what you're talking about. Some examples:

- "Ah, that's a European toaster. . . . I don't have the equipment to ground its internal circuitry."

- "Oh, man, I'd love to fix that, but it's illegal to open one up without a license. . . . Yeah, lawnmower engines contain trace amounts of radioactive material."

- "Yeah, I checked the septic tank. It's a bigger problem than just the toilet itself . . . it has to do with the city plumbing."

- "Sure I can fix that, no problem; do you know where the breaker-nine-series cables are for your home? It may be under the foundation."

- "Look, I just have a little trouble using an arc welder since that one exploded and killed my dad, okay? But I do know how to use one."

Dealing with Repairmen

Once you've made your peace with your family or roommates and called a professional to come fix whatever problem you're having, the exhausting adventure has only just begun. We don't want to make a sweeping generalization or a gross oversimplification, but anyone who will come to fix something in your home—be it a roofer, a plumber, or an electrician—is a fucking crook. There are no exceptions to this rule; repairmen evolved from ancient packs of roaming thieves. They'll clean you out for all you're worth if they see you as an easy mark, and nothing says, "Please rip me off," like a guy saying, "I dunno what the problem is . . . hot water just stopped coming out."

However, if you show some savvy, they're much less likely to charge nine hundred for caulking that hole in your roof. A little bit of knowledge may go a long way into convincing your repairman that you are no upper-middle-class sucker. Just know:

- If whatever's broken is supposed to be making things warm, like an oven, furnace, or water heater, make sure the pilot light is lit. If not, just relight it with a match or a lighter on your own and save yourself a ton of trouble and money.

- If something that's supposed to move has stopped moving (like your washing machine, dishwasher, etc.), the motor or one of the belts has probably gone out.

Other than that, you'll have no idea. Instead, look skeptically at the repairman whenever he gives you the diagnosis and the estimate. Any time he mentions a problem, raise your eyebrows and cock your head. If the estimate sounds high, and it will, say something to the effect of "It looked more minor to me; I might need to get a second opinion here." He'll respect your knowledge and your shrewd negotiations, and you'll get a cheaper price.

If that doesn't work, tell him you know another mechanic by the name of Benjamin Franklin who may be able to get you a lower price. When he realizes you are bribing him, tell him that you actually do know a mechanic born into a family of history buffs and that you are insulted that he assumed you were trying to bribe him. Threaten to sue unless he fixes what is wrong for free. Nobody wants a lawsuit like that hanging over them.

When You're Forced to Fix Something

Nothing's more humiliating for a man than when his excuses for why he shouldn't fix something fail, and he's forced to actually try to fix it. You'll walk up to that broken water heater in front of friends and family, and you will fail. Unless you think ahead.

To safeguard against other excuses not working, you're going to have to be clever. Buy a toolbox and fill it with tools. Now, take the box out into the street and throw it down as hard as you can five–six times. This way it will be dented and scuffed up; only pussies who can't fix things have perfect prissy little toolboxes. When the time comes, walk up to the broken appliance with authority, open up your toolbox and start rooting around in it. After a few moments of searching, yell, "Aw . . . fuck . . . where's that pipe wrench? Jesus Christ, I told you guys to stop borrowing my tools!" Everyone will start looking at one another, mentally trying to finger the tool thief. Now you can just say, "You know what? Fuck it. It would cost more to buy a new one than it would to call a plumber," and go to the phone and call a plumber before anyone can object. Not only did you get out of having to fix it, you've also sown the seeds of discord among your group. When everyone's a suspect, no one's innocent.

QUICK TIP: Technically, your Rolls-Royce is in the shop—as long as *shop* means the "dealership," and *your* means "anybody's."

Her Car Trouble—Act Knowledgeable

Most car troubles can't be fixed at home, that's why God invented auto mechanics. However, if your lady friend is having car problems, she is going to expect some level of expertise out of you beyond just "I have a yellow pages in the back, baby. Just choose the closest one and I'll drive you there at halftime." Regardless of what happens, you're going to tell her to see an auto mechanic to fix her problem. You just have to pretend like it was an educated suggestion or else she'll see you for the lazy idiot that you really are. Get in the car with her and give it a drive. If the car makes a noise, say, "Ah, that doesn't sound so good. Probably a timing-belt issue." If the car doesn't make a noise, say something like, "You hear that? It's sort of a really low-level whirring? That doesn't sound so good. I'd take it to a mechanic." If she asks you to fix it, tell her you would, but you left that plank of wood with wheels on it in your other pants.

The Undercover Mechanic

So your girlfriend's car is broken, and she keeps asking you to take a look at it. Doesn't sound so bad, but you don't know how to change the oil, much less check the engine timing or replace a fan belt. Well, that doesn't mean you can't make the repairs. Just arrange for her to leave for an afternoon to go shopping with a friend, see a movie, visit her parents, or something similarly lengthy. As soon as she leaves, take her car to a mechanic and tell him you're in a huge hurry. Have the mechanic fix the problem, pay him, and go home. Put on an old white T-shirt, and wipe down a greasy part of the engine with a rag. Now, rub the greased rag on your shirt, hands, forearms, and a swipe across the face. When she gets home, you'll look like her knight in grimy armor, and she'll never know you didn't lift a finger to do any actual work. But be considerate, don't throw your sweaty grease-stained shirt onto her face and say, "You owe me a chicken dinner, bitch."

QUICK TIP: Even though the only thing you can fix on a car is filling up the gas tank, doesn't mean that's always the problem. Also, you have some gas on your feet.

Cleaning a Girl's Car

For some of us, even the simplest tips are too difficult to fake our way through, and there's no way we can possibly fix anything to impress a young lady with our mechanical acumen.

If this is the case, you must cheat. The easiest way to establish a psychic link in her brain between you and mechanical know-how is to clean her car. This is no small task, though; it's a scientifically proven fact that along with girls' bathrooms, girls' cars are some of the most unexpectedly disgusting places in the universe. Old salads from 1997, term papers from freshman year, dead possums . . . it would not be surprising to find any of these items in a girl's trunk. Roll up your sleeves, throw away all the trash, vacuum out the interior, and give it a good wash. A coat of wax can be added in the event that you're really, really

After reading this book, you can successfully fake your way through the following surgical procedures: None.
Surgeries You Still Can't Perform: All of them.

trying to get laid. Now, you've shown that you're handy, but also domestic, by doing nothing more than plugging in your vacuum.

Breaking Her Stuff

Sometimes girlfriends get angry at their boyfriends when they don't prove themselves handy enough around the house. Yelling, "I wanna see YOU fix the kitchen sink, slut!" isn't a great way to prove her wrong. Instead, break little items around her house, like a lamp or a stove. But remember how you broke it. Then when she notices it's not working, just undo what

Fixing somebody's appliances is much easier when you know exactly how they broke. Just make sure you can physically undo any damage you inflict.

you previously broke. Make sure to throw in some handy quote like, "There's your problem right there." Then whisper, "Your boyfriend is a compulsive liar."

The Cool Man's Guide to Blogging

You probably think there is no such thing as a "Cool Man's Guide to Blogging" because blogging is inherently very nerdy. And you would be absolutely correct. But, if you do have a blog, not all hope is lost. There are certain rules one must follow to ensure that any sense of dignity you did have before blogging still remains.

Rule #1: Never blog about anything serious, ever. Emotional blogging is the absolute worst form of self-therapy. It's unbelievably pathetic to spill your beans into a diary that's accessible to everybody you know. Be a real man and keep your feelings bottled up inside—or purchase one of those pink fluffy diaries with a lock. Joke's on you, though; all the keys to those things are the same. Now, to see how you really feel about Sally Thompson . . .

Rule #2: If you're going to choose a domain name for your site, try to keep it to just yourname.com. It may seem cool to purchase Bestblogever.com or Blog-Diarrhea.com. But when a girl ends up asking you, "Oh, you have a blog? What's it called? Can I read it?" it's much more normal-sounding if you just say, "Oh, it's just my name.com" instead of, "Oh, it's actually called BustaBlogOnYourFace.com . . . it's . . . an inside joke."

Rule #3: Do not update your blog more than once a day, and even that is pushing it. Blogging once a day means you have too much free time on your hands, blogging fourteen times a day means you have too much dry semen on your hands. Everything in moderation.

CHAPTER 6

Fashion and Grooming

It's going to take more than just mechanical knowledge to impress people. No matter what you're saying, nobody's going to pay you the slightest bit of attention if you're wearing an airbrushed sweatshirt that loudly proclaims your fondness for a certain NASCAR driver. You may think it's shallow and materialistic that our society places so much emphasis on outward appearances, and that's certainly a principled stance for you to take. However, please quit spouting it from behind the counter of the coffee shop where you'll work until you're forty-five—you're getting spittle in our lattes.

Yes, the urge to get out of bed and spend the entire day in pajama pants and an old Vancouver Grizzlies T-shirt can be overwhelming, however, it's important to look your best.

Unfortunately, very few people are naturally gifted in the art of making well-coordinated outfits, and if we're just going by the statistics, chances are you're not one of them. Instead, you're forced to fake your way through the world of fashion relying solely on keeping each outfit so simple that there's no way you can screw things up.

A common pitfall you must avoid, though, is the that-looks-nice-on-you trap. It's happened to all of us; a girlfriend or female pal tells us a shirt looks great on us. For the next three years, we wear the exact same outfit to every date, party, or bat mitzvah we attend. Sure, the shirt may look good on you, but when it's become so tattered that you're patching the patches, it's probably time to diversify a little bit. Instead, fake your way to the same outfit by buying more shirts in the same color or cut; that way you're just a guy who really likes lavender, not the guy who never changes shirts.

Of course, anyone who's ever been to school with a rich Eastern European kid knows that the fanciest clothes in the world can't get you laid if you smell terrible. As such, you should put every bit as much time into your feigned grooming as you do into your threads. Shower every day (yes, even Tuesday), shave on occasion, and get a haircut. If you have bad acne, we suggest that you don't anymore; it's not going to help you any. When it comes to human maintenance, there aren't many corners you can cut. Swimming doesn't count as a bath. Chewing gum does not count as brushing your teeth. And your perspiration is not actually a French cologne. You will need to make some effort, but the little bit you will learn in this chapter will go a long way. Not unlike that toothpaste you've been milking since 2004. If you have to slice open the tube to get the last bits, just cough up the five bucks and get a new one; your gums will thank you.

Fashion Don'ts

The good news: You've finally managed to attend or graduate from an accredited four-year university of dubious academic standing. The bad news: It is often not socially acceptable to continue to dress like a student from an accredited four-year university of dubious academic standing. While banishing your ratty USC Cocks hat to the deep recesses of your closet may seem anathema to your carefully cultivated sense of style (that is, dressing exactly like your frat bros), it must be done.

What are some other sartorial no-no's? Glad you asked! Here's our definitive* list:

1. Striped shirts (specifically, with black pants. More specifically, with black pants and black shoes): "Are you loco?" you say, "A striped blue shirt with black pants and black shoes is my party uniform!" Yeah, well, it's the party uniform for four dozen other Johnny Cheesedicks in the bar as well, all of whom you're trying to distance yourself from in the eyes of that pretty brunette in the corner who looks bored out of her mind. Striped shirts are for accountants. Are you an accountant? Really? Fuck, man . . . our bad. Just don't give off that vibe when you go out.

---

*Not actually definitive.

2. Baseball caps: Briefly mentioned above, but bears repeating. If you're not actually playing baseball, don't wear one. Same goes for batting helmets. It's that simple. Yes, some black people can get away with wearing a cap cocked to the side; you most likely cannot. Sunglasses were invented for a reason—if your face needs shade, buy a pair. (Relevant side note: It's rather difficult to find a pair of sunglasses that don't make you look like an extra from *Zoolander,* so make sure you go shopping with someone whose aesthetic judgment you trust. Under *no* circumstances, though, should you buy a pair of . . .)

3. Oakleys, specifically with Croakies: This combination may be particularly hard to part with if you have spent more than six months residing below the Mason-Dixon line, but Oakleys with Croakies are so lame they might as well be sold together as a sex deterrent kit.

4. Asian-themed tattoos: That Chinese character above your left shoulder blade may say, "Tiger Warrior," but most people will likely interpret it as "Douche Bag."

5. Baggy jeans: There's a difference between "low rise" and "half my ass is showing." Ask a sales clerk if the jeans you're trying on actually fit. If they lie, most cities even have little wizards called tailors, who for a nominal fee will use magic to transform jeans that might be a little too long into just the right length. Make use of them.

6. Sneakers: If they're of functional use in an actual athletic endeavor, you probably shouldn't wear them out. Yay:

Chuck Taylors and Jack Purcells by Converse, Adidas Stan Smiths. Nay: cross trainers, basketball shoes, New Balances.

Interesting fact: The cap and gown were first used to hide recent graduates' ugly clothing. Refrain from wearing anything shown above after graduation day.

QUICK TIP: People who look cool in hats: Abraham Lincoln, rappers, baseball players. People who don't: everyone else.

Guide to Wearing a Suit

There's no denying it: Suits are magical. They can make any derelict look at least moderately professional, just by throwing on a blazer and a matching pair of pants. The most important thing is looking comfortable in your suit, but there are also certain rules that you have to remember so you don't look like an amateur. They are as follows:

- Never, ever button your bottom button. If you are wearing a three-button suit, you button the middle one. The top one can be buttoned as a matter of personal preference, but never without the middle one already buttoned. For a two-button suit, just the top button is fastened. Unbutton when you sit down.

- A double-breasted suit is always buttoned on the top button, but you'd better be damn well certain you've got the juice to pull off a double-breasted suit before buying one. On second thought, you don't have the juice to pull it off.

- Make sure your pants aren't too long. They should have a slight break in the fabric at the ankle, but you shouldn't have a ton of fabric piled up down there. Also, too high and you'll look like Milhouse. Your mom will still think you're cool, though.

- Go with socks that are the same color or a shade darker than your pants. Unless you're good at this stuff, don't try to get fancy with patterned socks; go with a flat color close to your pants.

- The most versatile suits are probably navy or gray, and if you buy a nice one, you can wear it up to three days a week with different shirts and ties. It's a common misconception that black suits are only for funerals. You can wear one during the day, but don't match a black tie to it. You'll end up looking like a cross between a Jehovah's Witness and Tommy Lee Jones in *Men in Black*.

- Very rarely is a suit going to fit you perfectly right off the rack. Just run it into a tailor and have him make the appropriate alterations. If you're already spending that much money on a suit, it's no use having it hang off of your body. Unless you're a scarecrow. Then your clothes aren't really supposed to fit. Or match.

- Do not, under any circumstances, attempt to make your own suit. Sure it looks simple, but after buying a twenty-five-yard bolt of linen, some thread, and a pair of scissors, you'll find yourself waist deep in fabric with no real end in sight and a funeral in thirty minutes. Sure you'll save some face by turning it into a nice, light shawl, but nobody needs to mourn in a 1994 San Francisco 49ers–replica jersey and a scarf. Your mother deserved better.

QUICK TIP: You know those Texas-style bolo ties with the strings and the sliding thing? You don't? Good.

Getting Discounts on Clothes

There are lots of downsides of living in the United States and not Morocco. Hashish is pretty hard to come by, hardly anyone

wears a fez anymore, and you don't buy your clothing from
street bazaars where haggling is normal. Instead, you go to department stores where the price on the tag is firm and nonnego-
tiable, right? Wrong. If you see a big-ticket item you like, you
can almost always get a significant chunk of the price knocked
off with a little bit of strategizing. The next time you see a coat
or a suit you want, try one of these:

- Find some small, insignificant flaw in some part of the
  item that would immediately get damaged with normal
  wear. Think the very bottom part of a coat you'd sit on,
  an inner liner, or something like that. Take it to a sales
  clerk and say, "I'd love to buy this, but I can't pay full
  price when it's got this problem." See this soda stain on
  the sleeve? Not yet you don't, but after a straw full of Diet
  Coke and some sleight of hand you will. You can get off
  up to 20 percent this way depending on the store.

- Look long and hard at the item in front of a salesperson
  and say, "It's nice, but it's just a bit much . . . are there any
  sales coming up?" If the item's going to go on sale in the
  next week or two, they'll either a) give you the sale price
  right then, or b) offer to hold it for you until the sale
  starts, then give it to you at the sale price. Either way, you
  can save serious money using this tactic. Then you can
  spend some of the savings on a greeting card that says,
  "Ha ha, I fooled you, chump salesman!"

- If a manager or store owner, or even a salesperson who
  works on commission, is helping you, they'll be desperate

to make a sale to get that four-dollar commission. You've got all the leverage here. Ask if they can meet you halfway on the price. They'll probably say no, at which point you should start leaving the store. Knowing that their sale is on the ropes, they'll probably give chase and cut you a better deal. Way to go, savvy shopper; now, go have a slice of Sbarro in the food court to celebrate.

Note: This doesn't work with food—next time you order a six-piece chicken nugget meal, don't ask them to level with you here. And that's not a ketchup stain on your hot dog, that's just the condiment you asked for, so you can stop playing hardball.

QUICK TIP: That's not a pocket square; that's a Rice Krispie Treat.

The Shoes Make the Fraud

As a nonincarcerated member of the community, you are afforded the luxury of paying attention to footwear. And attention you should pay: The right shoes tie your whole look together; the wrong ones make you look like your mommy dressed you. Here's a handy primer on how to avoid the latter:

1. With jeans and khakis: It's hard to go wrong with simple tennis shoes like Jack Purcells or Vans. Loafers and other brown shoes also work if the occasion is a bit more formal,

but save the wingtips for your suits and leave the square-toe black shoes for the guidos. And you no longer have to feign an interest in Greenpeace and patchouli oil to persuade coeds to sleep with you, so get rid of the Birkenstocks already.

2. When dressing formally, your shoes should be as dark as your suit. This means black shoes with black suits, black or dark brown shoes with navy suits, black or dark brown with gray. Yes, there are exceptions (if you're wearing sneakers or tennis shoes with a suit in a casual setting, for one), but there are exceptions to all rules, so stop nitpicking.

3. No-no's with shorts: sport sandals (Tevas and the likes), boots of any kind, or lace-up dress shoes. Slip-on loafers and boat shoes are your best bet, especially if you wear them sans sock for the salt-encrusted, wind-blown prepster look (which doubles as the this-is-Daddy's-yacht-but-I'm-inheriting-it look). Sneakers can go either way: Your fluorescent yellow Nike Air Shox are a bit much if you're not doing anything actually athletic, but simple Keds or the like work nicely.

4. Take care of your shoes. This is obvious, but often ignored. When your soles get worn down, take them to a cobbler to get resoled. Fix scuffmarks. Waterproof suede shoes before you wear them out and get stuck in the rain. Your shoes will last a lot longer if you treat them properly. Get a homeless guy to buff them for you, then kick

him when he's done. The buffing will make them shiny, and the kick will ensure nothing's stuck to the heel.

5. Know when to say good-bye. Proper maintenance can prolong your shoes' life but those Converses are starting to smell. People know they're the ones you wore in sixth grade because you've cut off the front so your toes could fit. If it looks like your feet have grown five inches in the past minute, time to get some new shoes.

Though shoes only spatially represent 10 percent of your outfit, they can easily ruin your entire appearance.

Socks: The Thinking-Man's Shoes

Some of us have absolutely no idea when it comes to fashion, but that doesn't mean you can't fake a little bit of flair in your wardrobe. Presumably you've taken the all-solid-colors-basics tactic when assembling your wardrobe, so spice up things a little with patterned socks. Stripes, argyle, polka dots, and twills can all make you look like you've got a funky eclectic vibe to your fashion sense, all without spending much money or taking any real risk of looking like an ass. As long as they don't clash with your shoes, like brown socks with black footwear, it's hard to go wrong.

Side note: If you want people to think you're anything other than a pubescent loser dressed by his mom, only wear white athletic socks when you're doing something athletic like going to the gym or playing sports. White athletic socks send a message of "I have no idea how to dress myself."

Dryer Sheets—The Best Five Bucks You'll Ever Spend

Contrary to what you may have learned in college, dryer sheets can be so much more than just something you stuff in a water bottle to poorly disguise the scent of marijuana smoke. Your mom's been throwing them in with the laundry for years, and she hardly ever smokes pot when she's doing household chores. Simply dropping a few dollars on a box of Bounce sheets can give you a ton of benefits. One, they soften your clothes and bed linens, so not only will you be more touchable, but anyone who ends up in your bed will be more comfortable and likely to stay there or return. Plus, dryer sheets smell nice, so they'll help your clothes cover whatever odors are emanating from your person. Finally, you'll seem like a guy who really knows how to do laundry, and acting like you've got a little domestic knowledge is never a bad thing.

The Free Haircut: Costlier Than You Think

There are three types of haircuts in this world: The first is the salon haircut that will cost you more in tips than the entire cut should; the second is the ten-dollar I-told-him-to-take-just-a-little-off-but-he-didn't-really-understand-English haircut; and then there is the free haircut.

The free haircut comes in many forms, but there is one common characteristic: It's always a bad idea. Any money you save will immediately be lost when you have to go buy a variety of hats to cover your dome, and no sombrero can cover this shame.

The self-haircut: Unless you plan on buzzing your head over a trash can, the self-haircut always seems like a great idea until you realize how difficult it is to cut the back of your own hair. The problem is, nobody has enough hand-eye coordination to figure out which way is which when your arms are over the back of your head and navigating through a triple-reflection-mirror setup. "This feels about right," you may think to yourself as you snip away, but it won't look anything close to right.

The girlfriend haircut: "What's the matter, don't you trust me?" Don't fall into her trap. If she thinks that anybody can cut hair, then why do they have barber schools, huh? Why do they have barber schools!? Odds are, she's trying to mess you up just enough so that she can still tolerate

Giving yourself a haircut may seem like a good idea, but it will usually leave your hair looking asymmetrical and your feet smelling like garbage.

looking at you, but any other woman who sees you will laugh and walk away. Cutting your hair is easier for her than installing a spycam in your room.

The barber school discount: Your locks are not a final exam, so don't turn your head into a hairy Scantron. Odds are, if they're cutting your hair for practice at a barber school, they're not used to succeeding much at life, and this is no different. Instead, why not skip a meal and save that ten-dollars for somebody who's already passed barber school with flying colors. Plus, if you sit still and don't wiggle—free lollipop!

What Your Facial Hair Says About You

Few physical affectations say more about you than the way you wear your facial hair. Are you funny? rugged? a struggling artist? done with puberty? Your facial hair, or lack thereof, provides real insight into the real you (if you're at a loss as to why parents grip their children tightly and cross the street when you approach, it's probably time to shave off the wispy 'stache, you fucking pedophile). Herein, what your facial hair says about you:

1. Cleanly Shaven No Facial Hair: A smooth mug indicates one of two things: The first is that you cannot actually grow facial hair, and are thus, with 80 percent certainty, Asian (whether you are in fact Asian, however, should be exceedingly obvious to anyone who pays you but the slightest of gazes. As such, we should note that shaving to

convey a spurious Oriental genealogical background seems an exercise in futility.) Alternately, being cleanly shaven, day in and day out, screams gainful employment at a bulge-bracket i-bank or consulting firm, and thus an income in the low six figures. Omit the whole thrice-weekly-existential-crises thing when whipping out your Amex at the bar and you're good to go.

Good for picking up: rich, gullible Korean girls; prenup-wielding trophy wives.

2. Five o'clock shadow: A no-no in most real offices, a few days of growth lets the world know that you are a brooding "creative" or, as they say in the biz, unemployed. (We're sure your friend's cousin's niece passed along your script to her boss at William Morris, so don't sweat it.) If nothing else, some thick stubble announces to the world that you heartily denounce the entire neocapitalist system of corporate whoredom as you head to the post office to pick up Daddy's rent check. Now back to work on that screenplay, dude!

Good for picking up: Trustafarian art students; coffee-shop baristas.

3. Goatee: What is this, 1997? Do you also have a favorite Hawaiian shirt for Casual Fridays, too? Ewwww. Shave that thing off immediately.

Good for: nothing.

4. Full-on beard: a toss-up. Beards look badass when they're grown in, but the intermediary phases can be pretty tough,

especially if you have to go to work for a week and a half looking like one of those scraggly dudes you see pissing on the subway at 2:00 A.M. There's also a fine line between "I am my own man" and "I chop wood for a living," so, unless you're self-employed, make sure you trim. If you are fortunate enough to make your own hours, grow that sucker out—you're golden once girls realize you're not a homeless rapist.

Good for: ensnaring crumbs; competing in the 2005 AFC Championship game.

5. Mustaches: We can safely assume that no twenty-something is making an earnest attempt to sport handlebars, so irony appears to be the guiding aesthetic for attempts in this category. As with most things of which irony is the guiding aesthetic, mustaches often look fucking ridiculous. Only about 3 percent of guys can actually pull off one without looking like they're either trying too hard or a kiddie pornographer; if you have to ask yourself whether or not you are part of that 3 percent, you're not. On the off chance that you can, it doesn't really matter: you're a style god and will probably get laid no matter what you look like. Asshole.

Good for: hipster trash; vaudeville fetishists.

QUICK TIP: If you are going to use a haircut vacuum extension to cut your hair, make sure to take it off before vacuuming. Unless you wanted to give your carpet a two with a fade.

Facial Care for Chumps

Taking proper care of your mug has become an unnecessarily complicated task. It used to be that a bar of soap and shaving cream were the only things you needed to put on your face each morning, but the clever cosmetics execs who popularized the word *metrosexual* would now have you believe that if you don't shell out for a sixty-dollar container of anti-aging facial crème derived from fish semen, you won't get laid. Lies! You're not getting laid for a variety of reasons, but using the wrong moisturizer isn't one of them. That said, a nice complexion goes a long way toward making up for your myriad other shortcomings, so there's no reason not to expend the minimal energy it takes to achieve one. Here's how:

Step #1: Use a face-specific cleanser. Yes, *cleanser* sounds like an effeminate euphemism for "soap," but the Ivory you use on the rest of your body will likely cause your face to dry out. You don't need anything extravagant here—just something to use morning and night that will wash dirt and other impurities from your pores. Experiment a little to find one that works for you, but generally speaking, those that contain glycerin (helps skin retain moisture) are good, and those that contain alcohol (leads to overdrying) are bad.

Step #2: Exfoliate depending on your skin type. Probably the step that helps the most that most guys skip. Exfoliating rids your skin of dead cells, makes way for new ones, and gives your face a healthy glow. If your skin is on the oily side, you can use a product with a mild abrasive more frequently than if your skin is dry. Some fancier scrubs contain things like bits of walnut or fruit, but those can be harsh on your face and aren't really necessary. Unless you're hungry.

Step #3: Find a moisturizer that works for you. The final step after cleansing and exfoliating. They put all sorts of crap in these things, but those containing shea butter, jojoba oil, omegas, and nut oils are particularly effective. Bonus points if you use one with UV protection. You should probably moisturize twice a day, but doing it once a morning should suffice. Moisturizing three times will make your skin too moist. People will notice and begin to tauntingly call you Moisty.

Remember, healthy skin may seem insignificant, but it's the only part of your body that people will see. Those who spend so much effort on a healthy heart or lungs are just improving unviewable organs, hidden below their opaque skin. Get your priorities straight, people.

QUICK TIP: Eating seven Altoids isn't as good as brushing your teeth. No, it's not an urban legend. You just made it up right now.

Book in the Back Pocket

You want instant academic cred? Take a paperback book, fold it, and cram it into your back pocket. This literary ass-handkerchief, too big to fit entirely in the pocket, pokes its head out and screams, "COOL," at the top of its lungs to anybody willing to hear it.

Where to wear it: Only a certain type of lady will notice your intellectual hemorrhoid, so choose your location wisely. Libraries, coffee shops, and bookstores are your best bet.

How to wear it: You're going to want to get a used copy that looks like you've personally worn it down. For extra cool points you should tear off the cover. If anybody asks, say it just gets in the way. Also, the book should be soft cover because you're going to be folding it in half in order to ensure it fits. (Though it was pretty impressive when you sawed that hardcover edition of *Gravity's Rainbow* and jammed it right in there.)

What book to use: Don't use *The Catcher in the Rye* or any other book you read in high school. Poetry is a pretty solid bet, except then you might be asked to explain it, and unless you have particular insights into Elizabeth Barrett Browning's sonnets, this will be too difficult. Try going into the bargain bin of any local bookstore and look for a famous author but an obscure title. Ever heard of Hemingway's *Islands in the Stream* or Faulkner's *Flags in the Dust*? Yeah, neither has your next girlfriend, but she still seems pretty damn impressed.

Special Note: If you're going to be using the book-in-back-pocket approach at impressing your literate crush, you're going to want to switch the book every couple of weeks. It may seem impressive that you're carrying a copy of Kerouac's *Dharma Bums,* but not when people realize it's taken you six months to finish a 250-page novel. (Although "You try read-

Keeping a book in your back pocket is a great way to subconsciously signal to girls that you are intelligent, when in actuality you don't know how to read.

ing with your butt and see how long it takes you!" will be a funny comeback.)

Stop Ironing Your Own Shirts

While a little bit of well-placed domestic skill can impress people, any advances you make here will be completely undone when they look at the wrinkled-up ball of a shirt you're wearing. If you are going to go to all the trouble of buying nice shirts, you might as well take them to the cleaners and have them professionally washed and ironed. They'll do a considerably better job than you will, and instead of spending what

It may seem simple because your mother used to do it quite easily, but ironing your shirts will turn into a bigger hassle than you thought.

seems like forever hunched over an ironing board as you try to flatten out each shirt, some laundress will do it for you. It sounds expensive, but in most cities it's well under two dollars a shirt. So next time you find two crumpled bills in the dryer, why not spend it on something that will make you look better, rather than a Chipwich? Just a thought.

CHAPTER 7

Caring for Your Home

Your faking up to this point must have been convincing, because now you've gotten a girl to come home with you. Unfortunately, the deal is far from sealed, as women and most other members of respectable society will be completely repelled by the fetid den you probably call home. Don't get us wrong, it's impressive that you somehow managed to cram a metric ton of garbage into a studio apartment. However, the smell is starting to get a little bit overpowering, and it appears those watermelon rinds in the corner are now supporting some sort of self-aware bacterial colonies.

These factors would seem to conspire against you in your efforts to seduce women, entertain guests, and avoid getting tetanus in your sleep. However, they don't have to, for you can fake your way to a presentable apartment with minimal expense and effort. By cutting the right corners, you can turn a pit into a hovel and a hovel into a dump! More advanced techniques can turn a studio into a spacious three-bedroom loft; you just have to figure out how to tear down sheetrock and incapacitate your neighbors, who will probably complain when you turn their bedroom into your study. You just need somewhere you can sit and think is all—is that so much to ask?

Having a clean, well-decorated place is among the easiest ways to make it seem as if you've got your act together. Once you get the trash out (and no, that's not a "collection" of empty pizza boxes; it's just a loose pile with a family of beavers living in it), you're halfway there. Depending on your particular level of filth, you can probably clean up the rest of the place with a solid afternoon's worth of work. Just a few hours a month can make a huge difference. If things are considerably nastier than normal human decency would accept, you may just want to give up and let the dirt stay. Plant flowers in it, and tell guests that it's all part of your plan to turn your home into a working garden. "Organic food you've grown yourself . . . that's the only way to eat." Reach down into the moldy sod and take a big chomp of a green pita so they'll know you're serious. "Delicious."

But if you do decide to clean up the place, you'll need to spend some time decorating it. Your first impulse may be to toss up a poster of a girl in a bikini, your college diploma, or a poster of a girl in a bikini holding up your diploma (possibly the only perk of attending Arizona State). Fight this urge, and it will pay off later. Instead, look for some tasteful furniture, some interesting prints or paintings for your walls, and a giant mirror above your bed. (Rap stars have them so they can get a bird's eye view of themselves in bed alone reading Russian literature—it's very classy.) One last point, though. That's not a print. That's a poster of Linkin Park. You can tell because instead of looking like a painting, it looks like a photograph of every member of Linkin Park walking down an alley. Switch it out for a nice Monet, and you're golden.

Decorating No-No's

Most people get their first real grown-up apartment or home of their own right after college and are then faced with a conundrum: They've got this huge, awesome living space, but they don't really have anything with which to furnish it, much less decorate it. Many people resort to a hideous plan of nailing anything they can find to their walls to add some color to their rooms. This big mistake usually yields rooms that leave visitors feeling vaguely uncomfortable as they say, "Wow . . . a smashed guitar on the wall . . . that's . . . interesting. . . ." as they back slowly toward the door. Don't fall into this trap; just because you're short on cash and decorating sense doesn't mean you can't have tastefully appointed rooms that awe guests.

Points to Remember

- You may not be great at math, but remember this equation: Posters = Terrible. Posters were great in college; they covered your cinder-block walls ably, but those days have passed. Wow, what a cool periodic table of drink recipes;

does it have the element "Nevergetlaidium" on it? In the real world, posters are just going to make you look like you're stuck in some sort of arrested development. If you've signed a lease, you've agreed to pay your rent every month, but you've also implicitly promised not to put anything on the walls with Sticky Tack.

- Plants can do a lot for any room with a window. They're relatively inexpensive, and if you can keep them alive, your visitors, particularly ladies, will know that you are responsible and at least moderately nurturing. Don't go overboard, though. If you put a half-dozen plants in each room, it will get creepy pretty quickly. Girls want to visit a house, not Fern Gully. Side note: A cactus may be impossible to kill, but it's the botanical equivalent of having a pet snake. Guess you'll be listening to those metal records by yourself, cool dude.

- How to care for your black light: With black light in hand, walk to a window. Open window. Throw black light out. Sure, it may hit someone, but they'll have no problem sacrificing their body for the greater good.

- Anything that would look at home in a 1960s opium den should immediately be thrown away. These items include lava lamp; wall tapestry (no matter how awesome it looks with the Pink Floyd–album covers on those women's backs); beads that hang in doorways; Jim Morrison's body; and, of course, kilos of opium. Opium poppies can help you on the plant front, though, so keep them.

- No Salvador Dalí prints. Ever. It may not be a poster. It may be in a frame. It's still fucking lame. Oh, wow, you like Dalí? You and every other uninspired stoner douche bag from everyone's undergrad dorm. Yeah, Dalí's a wonderful artist who did a lot of important things. Merchandising *The Persistence of Memory* onto millions of low-quality prints wasn't one of them.

IKEA: Resist the Urge

There is no debate, IKEA is the cheapest and most efficient way to furnish your house. Ten-dollar end tables, forty-dollar lounging chairs, ninety-dollar beds, IKEA is so cheap you won't even care about the fact that you'll need to spend the next month assembling all of this crap. Their furniture is so inexpensive you'll begin to grow the desire for oddly named and unnecessary items. You didn't think you needed a KULEYBURNY or an EKTOTURP until right this moment—and now you want twelve!

There are two main problems with IKEA. First, their furniture is extremely flimsy and cheaply built. So if you're wondering why that coffee table only costs nineteen dollars, it's because it only cost them two dollars to make it. You shouldn't be able to lift coffee tables like that with one hand and use them to scratch your back. IKEA is like a background set in a play. It looks very nice, but if you give it a little push the entire backdrop will fall down. Similarly, if your IKEA sofa falls apart during a date, your facade will be exposed.

Second, everybody you know has had IKEA furniture. Which

means people will know exactly how cheap you are, because at one point in their lifetime they were that cheap, too. It may fly in college to spend $100 furnishing an entire living room, but now that may come across as a little too frugal. Oh, and you have a ramen stain on your futon, so you may wanna flip that cushion. Don't bother trying to scrub it; Oriental flavor is the hardest to get out.

So go to IKEA; get an idea of what you like. The showroom of coordinated model rooms gives you a good idea of how to work with real furniture, but don't purchase anything there. Other than, of course, 120 Swedish meatballs for $5.99. Man, you can't afford not to do that.

ÜGGLI

As you grow older you realize that "affordable" and "practical" furniture makes you seem "cheap" and "immature."

Decorating Your Bathroom

Most visitors to your home will spend most of their time in the living room and, if you're lucky, the bedroom. However, if you're having girls over, they'll inevitably want to use the bathroom. The bathroom is the grossest room in the house, but if you can give it some subtle dignity, it can up your standing in the eyes of people who "really hafta pee." The easiest ways to do this:

- Get some decent towels. Yeah, you've still got those awesome towels from college with your name embroidered on them, but unless you're still living in a dorm, nobody's going to confuse your linens with their own. Get some Egyptian cotton towels, which are particularly soft due to their long fibers, and people will notice. Especially that pharaoh's daughter you've been trying to impress.

- Match your bath mat to your new towels. It's not gay to have the most rudimentary matching in your bathroom. Now, if you're matching a fish-shaped bath mat to your towels, that will look like either a) you're interested in deviant sexuality, or b) your mom picked it out for you. A blue bath mat with blue towels is perfectly normal. A bath mat made of human skin to match your human-skin towels is pretty weird, not to mention woefully underabsorbent.

- You have to have something to read on the toilet. That's acceptable. But you know that September 2003 issue of

Maxim you've been keeping in there? The one where splash-back from the shower and toilet has made all the pages expand and get crinkly? Throw it away. Now. One, you shouldn't have a subsoftcore magazine in the bathroom when company comes over. Two, buy a fresh subscription, dude. Keep some sort of large, important-looking book or boring magazine like *Architectural Digest* in there. People will think you love learning so much that you can't even slow down to use the bathroom. For bonus points, put in

Flowers are a great way to liven up the bathroom, but instead of placing them in the toilet, try arranging them in a nice glass vase. Your guests will need a place to urinate.

some Post-it notes next to expensive furniture that you "want to build."

- People are going to look in your medicine cabinet. They shouldn't, but they will. Buy a pack of extralarge condoms and put it in there. Wait for the rumors to start.

- You may have to stick with your ultradandruff fighting shampoo, but that's no reason to advertise it to the world. Transfer it into a nondescript pump bottle you can get for a buck or two at any big chain store. Perfect. Just make sure that bottle isn't a water bottle; you don't want your blind girlfriend foaming lather all over you.

QUICK TIP: People call futons "flip and fucks," but if you're trying to seduce women on a futon, it's probably more like a "flip and masturbate while crying."

Cleaning Your Home

Having a house that looks clean and having a house that *is* clean are completely different things. Having a house that's actually clean is for old people. Looking clean, though, can seriously impress visitors. Nobody likes a slob; that's why Oscar the Grouch died alone. Here's a simple guide to making your house look cleaner than it is:

- Any time before you go out to a bar and there's a chance you could bring home a young lady, make sure things are tidy. Nothing fancy, just get the dishes out of the sink, make the bed, chase out any deranged gypsies who were eating the stuffing from your couch cushions, etc.

- Get some Formula 409 and a paper towel, and wipe out the inside of your bathroom sink and the surrounding counter-top. Since girls are always using the bathroom, they'll end up washing their hands at some point (although this point is debatable), and you don't want them to see dried tooth-paste caked in there. Don't worry about cleaning the shower, toilet, etc. As long as there's nothing growing in there, no one will notice. If there is something growing in there, tell visitors that it's going to be a miniature marsh ecosystem, and people pay more for toilets like that. They just don't know because they've got no class.

- Pick up all the clutter in your bedroom and living room. If you were actually cleaning, you would put this stuff in its proper place. You're not, though, so stuff it all in a drawer or closet. Make sure she doesn't open said closet, though, or she will surely get sucked in by the tidal wave of crap you threw in there and crushed by a veritable toy tsunami.

- Dust the major surfaces in your home, particularly any nightstand or bedside table. That lemon-fresh scent com-ing from your can of Pledge smells like premarital sex. And lemons.

That's pretty much it. Once you've taken care of clutter, made the bed, and cleaned the bathroom sink, you'll look like a fastidious housekeeper who keeps things clean even if you could make a sourdough starter out of the bacteria under your shower curtain. Nothing's quite as delicious as a Frisco Burger.

QUICK TIP: If you run out of liquid dish soap, refill the bottles with green strawberry Kool-Aid. It will look roughly the

The first step to making your home presentable is to make sure you are the only inhabitant, human or otherwise.

same, and the look of horror on your friends' faces when you take a swig of that Palmolive will be well worth the twenty-nine cents.

Magazines to Leave Sitting Around

Simply having a well-furnished house or apartment isn't going to be enough to convince visitors that you're the sort of sophisticate they should admire. You'll still need to add some intellectual affectation to trick them into believing you're the sort of person who sits around thinking about currency crises rather than yelling, "Aw, shit!" at *Judge Judy* reruns. The easiest way to play up this facade is by planting magazines of culture, taste, and scholarly insight (read: those you don't actually read) around your home. Some of the best are:

The Economist

How to Use It: It's British, so you can claim that it "provides news without American bias." You can also claim that the always-unfunny cartoons on the cover are subtly subversive when they are, in fact, pretty stupid.

Potential Downsides: British spellings will begin to seep into your skull. Nobody wants to read about the colour of labour.

The New Yorker

How to Use It: The greatest pretentious magazine of all time, it lets you drop such gems as, "W. S. Merwin's last name may be

German for 'Merlin,' but his poem in this week's issue is less than magical." Chuckle condescendingly. You're so in.

Potential Downsides: Particularly stupid visitors will point out that you don't even live in New York.

The Atlantic Monthly

How to Use It: Spend three weeks getting through a 10,000-word feature on the failure of American troops to adequately dispose of Sunni insurgents in Iraq.

Potential Downsides: Devoting three weeks of your time to a single article.

Timothy McSweeney's Quarterly Concern

How to Use It: Impress that girl who's individualistic and artsy in the exact same way every other hipster is individualistic and artsy.

Potential Downsides: Spending $23 on a magazine means you'll have to start spending $109 on books. It's all relative.

Variety

How to Use It: Nothing suggests you're in the know about the entertainment industry quite like a daily rag with unintelligible headlines.

Potential Downsides: If someone asks, you'll have no idea what the headline "Mouse House hoofer's spex find new legs on fall sked" means.

Fake It with Flowers

Colorful flowers can brighten up even the most dank of abodes. They are relatively inexpensive and show that you're not a complete cretin; they only look effeminate if you make some huge elaborate arrangement. A few stems of a single variety, with the tips cut off at an angle and put in a simple vase of water with some sugar or Sprite in it, will wow the ladies. A couple of notes:

- Almost any flower other than carnations will work. Tulips, gerber daisies, or a few roses are pretty tough to screw up. Carnations can be expensive and quite nice, but visitors will automatically assume they're cheap.

- Go to a thrift store and get some cheap vases. They'll be fifty cents or so. This way, if a young lady comes over and goes crazy over your flowers, you can say, "Here, why don't you take these?" at the end of the night. You don't want to do that with some vase you paid thirty bucks for, and unless she's an expert on the Ming dynasty, she won't know the difference, anyway.

- Don't draw attention to the flowers. Act like they're there all the time because you just like to have a little color and beauty in your life. If a guest compliments them, casually respond with something like, "Yeah, they were just too pretty to pass up."

If you don't know anything about flowers, just choose the ones that look the prettiest but make sure to find out what kind they are. That way, "I dunno. Purple?" isn't your default response when a lady asks you what type of flowers they are.

Cooking for Yourself

An important part of a healthy domestic life is being able to cook for yourself. This way, you won't be snarfing down entire medium pizzas for breakfast, entire large pizzas for lunch, and calling the pizza place and asking if they can join two of the large pans together (don't worry, you'll totally pay double) to make some sort of extralarge pizza for dinner. Cooking for yourself will help you lose weight, and the maturity it displays will help lure in women. Unfortunately, cooking requires both talent and time, so you've been having most of your meals out of boxes, bags, and the occasional bucket.

This shortcoming doesn't mean you can't make people think you were cooking for yourself, though. Just fake it by lying. When someone asks what you had for dinner last night, say you got a great deal on some truffles and whipped up a little risotto. Constantly refer to things you just cooked for yourself, the more complicated the better. "Yeah, I'd had a rough day, but I had a free half hour so I whipped up a little Baked Alaska." Nobody wants to hear that you had Instant Noodles for dinner again; it's getting a little depressing. Spend your time hanging out in a Williams-Sonoma, and learn the names of kitchen products you should be using and food you should be eating. "If there were a fire in my house, the first thing I would save is my double balloon whisk. I'm nothing without it. Second is my saffron, and third, I don't know . . . old family photos I suppose."

Cooking for yourself is more difficult than it seems, oftentimes your favorite ingredients don't make for a good stew.

People will soon assume you are an accomplished at-home cook. Little do they know the only sous chef you've ever worked with was Hamburger Helper. And for him, a high five is literally a slap in the face.

Hiring a Live-in Maid

Cleaning, mopping, scrubbing, polishing, washing, vacuuming. Some people don't have enough time in the day to bother with all of these necessary gerunds. So you can do what any reasonable upper-middle-class family does: Hire a live-in maid.

"But I only have a 200-square-foot studio, do I really need a—" Let us interrupt you there. We know what you're going to ask, and the answer is yes. Sure, you can bring somebody in once a week and have her really tidy up the place, but what then? What happens the other six days as dust collects, as dishes pile up, as trash begins overflowing from the can and onto the floor? Are you going to pick it up? We should hope not!

"Seriously, I can't afford that. You're being unreasonable." Even though a live-in maid may cost more than your current salary, hiring one is always a great idea. Yes, she will keep the place perpetually tidy, but she will also go shopping for you and cook you food—provided you have enough money to afford luxuries like ingredients. Besides, think about how much money you are saving not buying other products, like an alarm clock or a live-in chef!

"But where will she sleep, I only have one bed, one couch, and a TV!?" Good. Now you're asking logistical questions. She will sleep on the floor; she's fine with that. In fact, she prefers it! Honestly, don't even stress out; it's good for her back.

"Listen, I need you to leave or I'm going to call the police."
Okay, fine. But we brought somebody here that we think
you should meet. Rosemary? Can you come in here for a
second? Rosemary's husband is sick and struggles to make
rent. She can't even afford public schooling for her children.
(Yes, the classes are free, but the pencils and looseleaf paper
aren't.) We told Rosemary you would hire her because our
points were so valid you would have no reason not to. But if
you want to fire Rosemary, just go ahead and do it, you
heartless monster.

"Okay, fine. I'll give her a week. But if that doesn't work out
then she's out of here! I'm serious!"

Another satisfied customer.

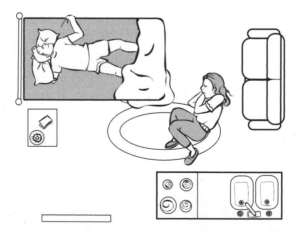

Don't worry about sleeping arrangements when choosing a live-in
maid. She's comfortable anywhere.

Prints Not to Hang in Your Home

1. *The Starry Night*

2. *Dogs Playing Poker*

3. *Dogs Looking at* The Starry Night

4. The Starry Night *Playing Poker*

5. *Reservoir Dogs* (playing poker)

– CHAPTER 8 –

Entertaining Guests

In college, throwing parties was easy. You'd get a keg of some light beer or a few cases, fill up your bathtub with ice to keep it cold, and send around an e-mail about a "total fucking rager. Dolphin House. Wednesday. Till Friday. Down with Homework." Scantily clad women would show up, and you would proceed to play beer pong until you threw up in the bushes.

Adult parties are markedly different. You have to buy a bunch of high-class liquor and send out an Evite advertising your sip and quip. Expensively clad women will show up, and you will play wine pong until you throw up on a zen garden. It will be a classier, more expensive vomit, and that will make all the difference.

Yes, as frat parties fade in importance for all but the most desperate of seventh-year seniors, it's time for you to start throwing some grown-up parties at your place. You can have a few friends over for cocktails, or you can throw a full-on dinner party. Whatever you do, it should send the message of "Hey, I'm an adult who can entertain friends in a sophisticated setting," so no serving Pez as finger food. (Yes, it's small enough, but even if you get the most dignified dispenser you can find—baby chick with a top hat emerging from an egg—your guests' teeth will get sore after their first roll of grape.) Still, with minimal expenditure and some artful faking, even you can have a classy soirée in your home. If you're thinking about what kind of cover you should charge, you should probably stop trying to make friends; nobody's going to like you. Have you considered becoming a sleazy party promoter in Daytona Beach?

There is only one rule to remember when entertaining in an adult situation: If it seemed like a great idea in college, it is now a horrible idea. This sentiment includes, but is not limited to, funneling beers, tapping kegs, and taking midterms. Instead, just try standing or sitting around and talking. Don't worry, people will still be drinking continuously, so there's no diminished chance that you'll have someone spend the night. However, you don't have to take off your shirt and refer to yourself as "The Omega Stud" to make this happen anymore; some witty banter will work much better.

Of course, if you're going to have all of this classy liquor, you might as well learn how to make some suitable drinks with it. Rum and coke may not reek of sophistication, but it will be significantly better than that chocolate martini recipe you made up, so don't get too fancy. Seriously, vodka poured into a melted Hershey bar? You thought someone would drink that? Learn how to whip up a few decent drinks people haven't had a million times before, and you'll become a great bartender according to everyone you know.

Finally, don't be intimidated about having guests over. Inviting people into your home shows that you're confident enough in your culinary and hosting abilities to take on a challenge, and people will generally be happy with free booze and snacks, no matter how they taste. Unless you give them all food poisoning. Then, you're on your own.

Cooking for Guests

The easiest way to impress guests, especially girls, is being able to cook. At this point, you're probably saying, "But wait a minute . . . I can't cook anything more complicated than Pop-Tarts, and the ones with icing are still too tricky for me." To which we say: "Of course you can't." It doesn't matter. Unless they've been to culinary school, almost all young men are terrible cooks. Girls will still give you points if you cook for them. Part of the points comes from the effort, and if you do it confidently, girls won't be able to tell you have no idea what you're doing. Have you looked at the crap they eat? Power bars, limp salads, skinless chicken breasts. You don't have to be that smug bastard Wolfgang Puck to win over a girl with your cooking. You just have to be marginally better than the line cooks at your local Applebee's. With the right attitude and easy recipes, you can fake your way through the kitchen and straight into the bedroom.

Throwing Cocktail Parties

Nothing sounds as dignified and classy as a cocktail party. But you have no idea how to throw a successful one. Fear not—it's easier than it sounds. To prove just how easy, we had a female friend arrange for seven girls we'd never met to come to our office after work. Our plan was to impress them using only our rudimentary knowledge of cooking, poor grammar, and cut-rate dental work.

Step 1: Get supplies. Most important, make sure you have the right sort of glasses for whatever you're serving. It's not that young ladies won't be impressed by your Mayor McCheese glass, it's just that most of them prefer something in a nice Fry Guy. If you're saying, "Wait . . . I don't have cocktail glasses or champagne flutes," quit your whining, baby. Go to a thrift store, where you can pick them up for a quarter apiece. Don't worry about everything matching; mismatched stuff done intentionally looks funky and chic.

Step 2: Figure out a menu. The key here is to pick things that look impressive or interesting but require very little cooking and can be prepared ahead of time. This way, if anything turns out to be a complete disaster, you can just throw it away, and nobody will be any the wiser.

Please note that a bowl of Doritos, even if the Ranch is Cooler than normal, won't work here. For our party, we tried:

Prosciutto-Wrapped Cantaloupe

- Buy a cantaloupe. Cut the inside flesh into one- to two-inch thin pieces. Tightly wrap each piece with prosciutto. If necessary, hold in place with a toothpick. Making thirty of these takes about ten minutes, and the salty/sweet combination is like a flavor orgasm in your mouth.

Stuffed Dates

- Get some dates (the fruit, not the March-2-1984-and-June-6-2001 kind). Cut them long ways like a hot-dog bun, pull out the pit, and fill the middle with cream cheese. Chop up some pecans, walnuts, or almost any noncorn nut into very fine bits. Roll each date in the chopped nuts. You're done.

Mango Guacamole

- For some reason that scientists still haven't pinpointed, most girls can eat pounds and pounds of guac without gaining weight or saying anything interesting. Get two or three Haas avocados (the good ones are dark green and just slightly mushy when you squeeze them), cut them open, toss the pit, peel, and dump into a bowl with some chopped onion, jalapeno, and a tiny bit of cilantro. (Don't use too much of any of this stuff. You can add more later if you want.) Toss in a handful of small mango bits. Mash with a fork until it's creamy and well mixed, then add sea salt, a pinch of cumin, and the juice of two limes. This will get you laid. Twice. In a row. Serve with tortilla or pita chips.

All of these things are easy, impressive, and can be prepared beforehand in ten to twenty minutes.

3. Choose your drinks. Everyone knows the standard lineup of heavy-hitter cocktails like martinis and whiskey sours. While no one will thumb their nose at you for serving or drinking one of these time-tested favorites, there's also very little chance anyone will be impressed by your knowledge of cocktails. Furthermore, if you're having company over for drinks, you want them drinking heavily, especially if not everyone knows one another. Martinis are loaded with alcohol, but they're by no means easy drinking. Instead, try something sweeter with less alcohol, which will make it easier to take big swigs.

For something that uses a cocktail glass, try making:

Lychee Martini

> *3 ounces of vodka*
> *½ ounce lychee juice or syrup*
> *1 lychee, peeled and pitted*
> *Mint leaves*
> *Tacos (for garnish)*

Shake the lychee juice and the vodka with ice and strain into a chilled cocktail glass. Garnish with the lychee and a mint leaf. If you're feeling particularly daring, drop a taco or two in the glass to take the flavor south of the border. *¡Muy bueno!*

For something that will subtly melt girls' minds:

Pimm's No. 1 Cup

Pimm's is an old gin-based liquor from England that has spices and coloring added to it. This punch-type drink was hugely popular in mid-twentieth-century London. Then again, so was fighting in world wars, and we're not recommending that. Yet.

In a tall glass with ice, pour roughly one third full with Pimm's and top with lemonade. Add a strawberry and slices of lemon, orange, cucumber, and apple. This tastes like it has no alcohol in it, but your guests will start to feel it after three.

For something that will taste like delicious candy but still fuck you up:

Strawberry Hard-Lemonade

Making strawberry-infused vodka is both easy and impressive, and we'll describe the process in a few pages. Pour about two ounces of strawberry infused vodka per glass and top off with lemonade. Add lots of ice. This will taste both delicious and alcoholic, like some sort of five-year-old bartender sold it to you for five cents. Add a strawberry to every glass for aesthetic purposes.

Music

Every cocktail party needs some music to fill in the awkward silences. Have some light airy sounds playing throughout the party, nothing very loud. And no, the Beastie Boys are not light and airy no matter how many acoustic versions of "Body Movin'" you have. Really? Fifty-two? Jesus, maybe you can make that work.

Ambience

Once you have the proper snack table set, the drinks being poured and the music playing, people will then begin to cluster up into groups of two to four familiar friends. It is your job as host to walk around and try to merge these groups as much as possible. Bring one person from one group into another conversation. You will know the most about everybody there, so it is up to you to facilitate this mingling. If there are any strays by the table mingling with only the guacamole, it's important that you get them away from your finger foods. Your party depends on it, and nobody's going to want to talk to them if they've got guac stains on their shirt.

That's about it. It may seem like a chore, but a well-orchestrated cocktail party takes about as much effort as any other party would, and it's ten times as impressive. Now, try not to hurl, you've had a lot to drink.

Infusing Your Own Vodka

Another way to get away with fairly cheap booze while still knocking peoples' socks off is to infuse your own vodka. Infused vodkas can take on the flavor of fruits, herbs, or spices; you're basically making your own Citron or Razz, but a) it's got a pretty color and b) it's impressive that you did it yourself. It's the easiest thing in the world:

1. Get a bottle of moderately priced vodka, whatever fruit you want to use for an infusion (pineapple, orange, lemon, strawberry all work well), and a jar with a tight lid.

2. Cut up some fruit (use around a pound . . . if it's too strong later you can just pour in more vodka), and put it in the jar. Pour the vodka in.

When infusing vodka, it's better to use sweet fruits like lychee or strawberries and not salty meats like bacon or pork chops (shown above).

3. Put the lid on and stick in a cool dark place for a week or so, like a closet, cavern, or abyss/metaphorical chasm.

4. Remove all the fruit and strain out any particulate crap left in the vodka with a coffee strainer.

5. Serve to your obviously impressed guests.

Added bonuses: You seem like a trendy vodka bar, when all you really did was spend an extra three bucks on fruit to make your sort-of-cheap sauce taste better. The total work involved here is under fifteen minutes, but no one will know that.

Refilling Liquor Bottles

You may think good parties are merely about finger foods, mood lighting, and song playlists. However, no amount of chicken satay, line dimmers, or *Pure 80's* Vol. 12, will compensate for cheap liquor. As such, you should only serve the finest top-shelf liquors at your parties. It shows that you have money and you're not reluctant to spend it on the enjoyment of your friends and acquaintances. Any vodka below Grey Goose, any gin below Bombay, or any fortified wine below Thunderbird is completely unacceptable to a sophisticated crowd.

This doesn't have to be as expensive as it sounds. Peoples' palates aren't as well tuned to tiny differences among spirits as they'd like to think. They assume Ketel One is a delicious vodka because it comes in a nice bottle and is expensive, not because there's a perceptible difference in its taste. As such, what you really need are the bottles of these liquors. Find empty bottles somewhere, perhaps by buying an initial bottle of the good stuff as a fixed-cost capital investment. Then, when you have parties, just buy whatever crap they're selling in plastic handles at the liquor store and refill your top-shelf bottles with it. For the price of two moderately priced handles as most people serve, you can get one great handle and one terrible one. After that, you save money every time you refill the good bottle with cheap booze. Your parties will quickly gain a reputation for having the best booze around, and you'll start to pull in more attractive members of the opposite sex.

If you are refilling your expensive bottles with cheap liquor, you should refrain from using gasoline—your guests will notice.

The important thing, though, is you've done it for pennies on the dollar.

(Please note: Unless you have a full-scale canning line that can reseal and carbonate 12 oz. cans, this tactic is considerably less effective for beer.)

Ask an Expert—Spirits Advice

Regardless of how well you are dressed and how confident you appear, if you're not drinking something to match your level of aesthetic sophistication, you may as well be at home in your boxers drinking a Squeeze-It in front of your TV. Unfortunately for you, the world of spirits (liquor, to the rest of us) is as intimidating as the attractive ladies you are trying to impress.

Fortunately for you, we spoke to New York City spirit sommelier Ethan Kelley, who runs the Brandy Library in Tribeca, about the comprehensive world of whisky and cognac. He knows everything there is to know about spirits and imparted the most useful, easy-to-share information with us. The first things you'll need to know are some general definitions:

"The spirit world is divided up into two main categories, whisky and brandy," Kelley explained as if he were teaching a sophisticated kindergarten class with a drinking problem. "It's as simple as beer and wine. If you ferment grains, you get beer. If you distill that beer you get whisky. If you ferment fruit, you get wine. If you distill that wine, you get brandy." Seems easy enough. So where do cognac, scotch, and bourbon fit in?

It's easy to remember:

Cognac—By far the most famous brandy, it is named after
    the commune in France where cognac is made. It is a
    grape-based spirit favored by rappers and other assorted
    ballers. Bourbon—A type of whisky made in America
    with at least 51 percent corn in the mash. Scotch—A type
    of whisky made in Scotland. There are two main kinds of
    Scotch: single malt and blended.

If you are explaining what you've learned so far to somebody,
their next question will be "What's the difference between single malt and blended?" If you want to seem like an expert, this
is how Mr. Kelley responded:

"This is sort of a soap-box issue for me, but everyone wants
to say that blended Scotches are boring. Without blended
whiskies being generous and kind enough to buy massive stock
from single malt distilleries in order to blend their own, those
single malt distilleries would go out of business in a heartbeat."
A drunken, Scottish heartbeat.

Sure, this doesn't explain what single malt or blended malt
whiskies are, but now you sound passionate and thus knowledgeable about spirits. And to think, thirty seconds ago you
thought whisky was just what made your mom leave your dad.
But just in case somebody calls you out on it:

Single Malt—Whisky made from one distillery. The Glen-
    livet would be an example of a single malt Scotch.
Blended Malt—Whisky mixed and matched from many dis-

tilleries. Johnny Walker Black Label is an example of blended malt Scotch.

Basically, the makers of blended whisky go around to a lot of little distilleries making single malts and buy a barrel here and a barrel there, then blend them all together to get a consistent flavor. A blended Scotch may have whisky from up to forty different distilleries in it. It's like science, but for drunk people.

So now that you know the background information, you're ready to start drinking! It's important to remember that, unlike high-end call girls, price does not always equal quality in the spirit world. Kelley says, "People who want to spend twenty-five dollars on a pour can come in here and I can give them something for twelve, fourteen dollars a pour that's better or of equal value." With prices that low, you can't afford to be sober!

"An example of this is Johnny Walker Blue Label. Most people who don't know much about Scotch see the $200 price tag on a bottle of Johnny Walker Blue and think to themselves that this is a quality whisky. What they don't realize is that the base malt of Johnny Walker Blue is Royal Lochnagar, a Scotch which costs roughly 20 percent of what you would pay for Johnny Walker Blue. When people purchase Johnny Walker Blue, they're not paying for the quality, they're paying for the marketing. It's a great Scotch, but so is Royal Lochnagar, which you can get that for about thirty-five dollars a bottle."

Most bars will have dozens or even hundreds of types of

whiskies and brandies. How will you know what type you will like? Kelley says to "Drink what you shot in college. So if you're used to drinking Jameson and ginger, cut it down to a splash of ginger, over time get rid of it all together." A good spirit takes time to get used to. Find your favorite, not necessarily the most expensive one. If you're really insecure, though, your favorite will probably be the most expensive one. Now you're looking good, champ!

Crying when you drink scotch is usually a sign of alcoholic immaturity or perhaps that your father was killed by a Scotsman.

And as for the drinking itself, Kelley says to enjoy all spirits the same way: slowly. "Sip it. Small sips. Take your time. This is something that should not be drunk inside of ten minutes. You should be able to take your time and enjoy it. If you want to have a cigar with it, have a cigar. If you want to eat a little something, a lot of this stuff goes great with various fruits and even chocolate; you can pair it up, but do not rush it."

You seem classier already. Or maybe just drunker. Either way, you're more of something!

Famous People Who Drank Each Cocktail

Occasionally, you'll want to have seven drinks without having people think you're some lowbrow roustabout. The easiest way to do this is by establishing yourself as an aficionado of fine spirits who knows his histories, which you can do by casually tossing off the name of someone famous who imbibed or wrote about each drink. These fall into roughly two categories:

Tom Collins—J. D. Salinger, who mentions the drink in both *The Catcher in the Rye* and the novella *Raise High the Roof Beam, Carpenters*.

Anything but Tom Collins—Hemingway. You can tie Hemingway into at least the following: grappa, the daiquiri, absinthe, cognac, Chianti, Spanish wine, the montgomery (a very dry martini), and just about anything else you can wrap your lips around. You can't ever go wrong with

Telling people, "This is what Ernest Hemingway drank every day of his life," is more convincing when you aren't about to beer bong a forty.

crediting Hemingway for sparking your interest in a beverage. People will think you're well-read and urbane; you'll know that you're just drunk.

Note: If you ever find yourself below the Mason-Dixon line, substitute Faulkner for Hemingway for similar results.

QUICK TIP—Champagne Versus Sparkling Wine: Although the terms are used interchangeably by most people, "champagne" is really only made in the Champagne region of France. Anything else is sparkling wine. You should know this fact, but you should not under any circumstance share it without serious prompting. Everyone hates that guy who says, "Technically, this isn't really champagne." You don't want to be him. Trust us. If you encounter him, tell him that it's an accepted colloquialism and that nobody likes a semantics snob. He'll go home and fall asleep clutching his copy of *Wine Spectator* and sobbing.

Ask an Expert—Beer Advice

It's a common misconception that wine is the classiest drink around with Great Bluedini Kool-Aid a close second. Contrary to what most people think, beer can be a pretty sophisticated drink in its own right. We interviewed Steve Hindy, the president and founder of Brooklyn Brewery, one of the largest craft brewers in the country, and asked him everything you need to know to seem like you've devoted your whole life to beer. Acting knowledgeable about beer is what separates drunkards from connoisseurs.

If you want to seem well-informed about beer, the most important piece of information, says Hindy, is knowing the difference between ales and lagers:

Ales: Use top-fermenting yeast strains and warmer brewing temperatures. Generally, when people think "ale," they have English and Belgian examples in mind, but lots of world-class American ales are available, usually at a fraction of the price.

Lagers: Use bottom-fermenting yeast strains and a cold fermentation process known as lagering. These factors lead to clean, crisp flavors that can be quite refreshing. Big American breweries' beers are watered-down takes on pilsner style of lager, but Germany and the Czech Republic make world-class lagers that are complex and flavorful.

What Else You Need to Know

Glassware is important. As Hindy notes, "It's really an uphill battle here in the States. For some reason, bars like these stupid straight-sided shaker pint glasses. They're straight-sided so they don't hold a head well; there's no lip on the top to help support it. In order to really get the best sense of the aroma of your beer, the fragrance of the hop character in the beer, you need something that's kind of curved in a little at the top, something that focuses the fragrance and aroma coming out of the head." Make sure to repeat this verbatim on your next date to seem learned. It may help to write it on your napkin, but be sure to look up every once in a while to make eye contact. It's just good public-speaking etiquette.

Use good beer to give your parties some dignity. "It's fun to present beer with food," says Hindy. "I would have some sliced bread, cheese, and probably have a pilsner beer, a lager beer, an ale, or maybe a porter, and some appropriate cheeses like an aged gouda or a very sharp cheddar, maybe some stilton. Play around with those flavors and get people to taste that beer. Beer is fantastic with cheese." Serving beer at a party may make you seem like a rich frat boy. Serving nice beer and cheese makes you seem like a sommelier. A little bit of cheese can go a long way.

Talk the connoisseur talk. Sounding like you know what you're talking about with beer is probably simpler than it is with wine. You don't have to pick out any subtle black currant notes or swirl the glass. Instead, follow Hindy's advice for an easy first impression. "Take a look at the beer and sniff it. You can tell whether the malt is the primary character of the beer or the hops, and that comes through pretty quickly. A very hoppy beer is going to have a very floral aroma and a very malty beer is almost like cereal—sweetness that comes through to your nose." Even if you're not really right in your first impression, whoever you're talking to probably won't know any better.

Congratulations, you should now know enough about beer to survive a couple of bar dates. Though after seven of these dates, she'll probably want to go somewhere nicer . . .

Dealing with the Cops

Oh, man, your party got out of control, and now the cops are there. You should have known this would happen when you got that house next to the police station, no matter how cheap the rent was. Nevermind, now you're in this predicament, so how do you get out of it?

Your first impulse is probably to smack one of those "fucking pigs" in the face for trying to ruin your good time. Great idea! Nobody will break up the parties you'll be attending in jail. Unfortunately, you'll technically be the refreshments at these parties, so it may not be worth it. Instead, calmly answer the door after turning down your music. Be as polite as possible, and open with a line like, "Aw, sorry, is the music too loud?" Ninety percent of the time, the cops come because your neighbors have called to complain about music. Apologize to the cops, admit it was too loud, and promise to turn it down. They should leave at this point, and you can crank it back up.

The best way to deal with the cops is to plan ahead. For several hours before your party, make a series of fake complaints to the cops about the noise coming out of your apartment. As they make stops at your place before the party even starts, try to contain your laughter as you tell them, "Sorry about my annoying neighbors, officer; you can just ignore them for the rest of the night." When the party hits into high gear and your actual neighbors complain about the noise, nobody will believe their story. Those little neighbors who cried wolf will never know what hit them. (A thrown whisky bottle.)

QUICK TIP: You can pass off catered food as your own, but be reasonable. Nobody's going to believe you just whipped up some S'mores Pop-Tarts.

Throwing a Dinner Party

Any jerk with a credit card and a pair of pants can go out to dinner at a restaurant, but it takes a real man who knows what he's doing to make it at home. While you can throw some white bread, peanut butter, and Welch's grape jelly into a blender and call it a PB and J smoothie, you can impress more people with an easy, faked dinner. To prove our point, we asked seven girls from a large magazine in New York to come over for dinner. To prove this can be easily faked, particularly for two people, we waited until the last possible second to start cooking. When buying the ingredients, don't forget to buy condoms, because you'll be using them after dinner. (They're part of the dessert preparation.)

Cashew-Honey Green Beans

> *1 pound frozen whole green beans*
> *1 cup cashew halfs*
> *3 teaspoons honey*
> *2 tablespoons butter*
> *Salt and pepper*

Boil a pot of water, and dump the thawed beans in for just a minute or two, till they start to give a little but are still crunchy. Strain them in a colander, and quickly dump into a bowl of cold water. In a skillet, heat the butter on medium heat, and sautee the cashews by pushing them around in the hot butter. Slowly mix in the honey, being careful not to burn it. When the nuts are coated with honey and nicely toasted, drain the beans and dump them into the skillet. Toss them around until they're coated with the honey-nut mixture, add salt and pepper, and serve. This takes something gross (green beans) and combines it with something delicious (cashews and honey) to make a vegetable that almost anyone can eat without making a face.

Entrée: Some Sort of Fish

If this plan didn't sound like faking it before, it kicks into high-gear now. Go to a local high-class yuppy market or caterer. Buy a few of the tastiest-looking fish entrées, maybe some nice salmon, maybe some halibut. Bring it home, destroy all bags, containers, and packages, and transfer the fish to a baking dish of your own. Put it in the oven on low heat "just to keep things warm." Now it looks like you made this delicious fish! Way to go; you're a regular gourmet!

The logic here is twofold. First, the entrée is the most important part of the meal. Even if your sides suck, people will remember the entrée. If it's not edible, they'll go home hungry and cranky. Furthermore, entrées are difficult to make. They require the kind of culinary skill that you probably lack if you're reading this book. However, opening your wallet and purchasing something supertasty? That requires nothing but money, and you've got that! Plus, it saves preparation time, so go catch up on your *Blossom* reruns.

Dessert is the most crucial part of the meal, and it's where you'll really seal whether or not you get to spend the rest of the evening with your guest. Pull out all the stops with something impressive looking but easy to make. Nothing fits this bill quite like:

Chocolate Bowls with Berries and Cream

> *1 bag good-quality chocolate chips*
> *Strawberries*
> *Blueberries*
> *Raspberries*
> *Whipped cream*
> *Water balloons (really)*

Blow up ten or fifteen of the water balloons with your mouth. In a microwave-safe bowl, nuke the chocolate chips for a minute and half. When you take them out, stir with a spatula. As you stir, they should start to melt into one big bowl of semihot liquid chocolate. Put some wax paper on a cookie sheet. Now, hold a balloon by the knot and dip the opposite end into the bowl of chocolate. Roll backward and forward, then right to left, until the bottom end of the balloon has a small layer of chocolate on it. Pick up, and set top-down on the wax paper with the knot straight up in the air. Keep doing this until you're out of chocolate. Put the cookie sheet in a fridge or freezer and let sit for four to five hours. Once the chocolate cools and hardens, use a pin to pop the balloons. Then, gently peel out the balloon, which should come pretty easily. You now have an edible bowl made of chocolate. You have to make quite a few to get a couple of pretty ones, but these are easy and superimpressive. Fill with the berries and cream and serve.

Remember to allot yourself a couple hours from cooking to dinner. If you rush it, people will be able to tell because you'll be sweating, and your apron will be burning. "On fire?

Me? No, it's just really bright in here. What's that? No, I did not cook human flesh for dinner. Actually, can you excuse me? I have to run into my swimming pool at full speed now."

QUICK TIP: No matter how delicious it is, nobody wants to eat food cooked in a garbage can. Yes, even if you rinsed it out first.

Kitchen Gadgets to Impress People

Cooking is like Cartesian philosophy: Perception is reality. Even if you don't really know what you're doing, stocking your kitchen with the right gadgets can make people think you do.

- Pepper mill—Fresh-ground pepper always tastes better than the crap out of a carton, and the mill itself is visually appealing. The quickest way to make people think you're a real cook.

- Butane kitchen torch—Nothing's manlier than a source of fire, even if you purchased it at Williams-Sonoma. Use the blue flame on this sucker to caramelize the tops of crème brûlée, toast merengue, and make other easy-but-impressive delicacies that will get you laid.

- Whisks—Whisks are cheap and aesthetically striking. If you have a cannister with a bunch of them in it, it will look like you're a serious cook who needs a specialized whisk for each task. Scientists have still not found a practical use for a whisk that doesn't involve impressing girls.

- Knife sharpener—They say a dull knife is more dangerous than a sharp one, but they've apparently never been stabbed eighteen times by a blade that's been honed to a razor's edge on an electric kitchen sharpener. Real cooks are anal about their knives. You've been using this gadget to try to re-sharpen your Mach 3 blades, but no one has to know that.

- Citrus zester—While using it you can say stuff like "back in the day, I had to zest my own citruses. It took hours to zest them, but we zested them. Oh, we zested them good. Still with me?"

- Omelet pan—For whatever reason, being able to flip things in a pan impresses people. Get a small nonstick omelet pan with a matching spatula, and learn to flip an omelet. It beats Lucky Charms, and she'll be coming back for breakfast again and again.

- Green Tabasco—A drop or two makes almost any recipe taste better. Please note: does not apply to applesauce. Please note again: Do *not* serve any sort of applesauce.

- Copper-bottom pan—Because people, like raccoons, are impressed by shiny things. The bottoms are tough to keep shiny, but since you're not going to really cook with them, it shouldn't be too tough.

- Garlic in a hanging braid—Also useful for deterring vampire attacks.

Fancy kitchen gadgets like whisks are great to have around, but don't defend against flames very well. Instead, try water.

Appreciating Aprons

You may think they're feminine, but wearing an apron is far better than having flour all over your shirt when your guests arrive. Shell out a few bucks for a decent apron, but make sure it's fairly plain. Monochromatic or something with a stripe or two isn't bad. Anything too fancy will make you look like a lonely homemaker who spends hours shopping for aprons.

Anything with a slogan like "Kiss the Cook" will make you look like a sad suburban dad whose grilling skills can't make his kids love him. "Hail to the Chef," on the other hand, is classy as all hell.

Though slightly emasculating, aprons are a great way to ensure you don't get food on your chest and thigh area.

Learn to Play One Song

People are impressed by musical abilities. Sometimes parties will have stray guitars or pianos, and a partygoer will wow everybody with his acoustic version of the Mario theme song or a piano version of the acoustic version of the Mario theme song. That could have been you. Instead, you are standing in the back throwing turnips at people, like some sort of Luigi.

You may think without the necessary ten years of lessons and five years of jamming that you don't have the necessary skills it takes to play a couple songs on the piano or guitar. And you are right. But you don't need to play a couple songs, you just need to play one.

Any moron with opposable thumbs can spend a couple of days perfecting one song on the piano or guitar. You'll probably need an actually talented friend to teach you how to play that particular song. When party time rolls around feel free to preach what you've practiced. As people scream for an encore simply refuse. Tell them the party isn't "about you." Tell them you could "play all night if you had to" but that wouldn't be fun for anybody. This will come off as modesty and will impress people even more than the song did.

Congrats, Beethoven, you left them wanting more. Little do they know you have nothing left to give.

CHAPTER 9

Hitting the Town

From an etiquette standpoint, a stone statue would be the ideal man. Sure, he wouldn't bring much to the table in the way of conversation, but he would never, ever screw up and commit a major faux pas such as talking with his mouth full, or putting his elbows on the table (unless he was sculpted that way.) Being polite, under many circumstances, just means being silent. Doing nothing also ensures that you are doing nothing wrong.

It's important to understand that etiquette is essentially a collection of hundreds of arcane rules, so there's no way you'll be able to remember them all. The great bulk of them are completely counterintuitive and don't make any objective sense. Why on earth are you supposed to eat asparagus spears with your fingers? Why should you always walk in front of the woman when going up stairs even at the expense of looking up her skirt? When you break a wine bottle over a dude's head in a bar fight, why are you supposed to swing it overhand rather than sidearm? There are no answers to these questions. These are just the rules put forth by the tribunal of eccentric Englishmen centuries ago to spice up life and ruin it for the rest of us.

However, this confusion can be plied to your advantage. Any time you feel on edge about having committed an error, simply claim that you were acting according to an unknown etiquette rule. You're not the barbarian, your companion is. "Actually, it's customary to refer to a busboy as 'that Mexican' in his former El Salvador. I'm just making him feel more at home." She'll never know that you're lying through your teeth if you're proactive about bringing it up and resolutely state your case. Ask her if she ever even finished charm school. Whatever her response, say, "Figures."

Seems harsh? It's not. The rules of etiquette are constructs designed to distinguish the rabble from the refined, and if you game the situation correctly, nobody will know that you belong firmly in the rabble camp. Now, polish that monocle, dust off your top hat, and hit the town. Sure, you may look like Mr. Peanut, but he's the head of a large corporation like Planters. You can't argue with success.

Ask an Etiquette Expert

Samantha von Sperling is the founder of Polished Social Image Consultants, a Manhattan-based company that strives to make

Don Juans out of Joe Schmos by offering classes in everything from proper fork and knife management to ballroom dancing. We recently sat down with her to find out what's wrong with today's youth (a lot) and how to remedy the situation (keep reading). "Most American youth are positively boorish," says Von Sperling. "That's why I get most of my interns in Europe." Oookay. Here's what she recommends you do to try to buck that rep:

Career Advice

1. Don't assume that sending a resume by e-mail is enough. Print it out on nice stationery and send a hard copy. The extra effort will pay off and might make your potential employer forget the small fact that your résumé sucks in the first place. Plus, it will help the struggling heavy-bond paper industry.

2. Do your research. Google the company you're interviewing with so you have tangible talking points to refer to during the interview. If you're sending a cover letter, find out to whom you should be addressing your inquiry. Simply writing "Dear Sir or Madam" in lieu of an actual name shows that you're lazy. Wait until after you get the job to emphasize that particular character trait of yours.

3. Create a professional-sounding Google or Yahoo e-mail account for work-related correspondence. Unfortunately, the Ballz69@hotmail.com address you've been using since you were downloading nudie GIFs with your dial-up modem is no longer acceptable.

4. A few days before the interview, brainstorm questions you think you'll be asked and jot down the answers. This will plant seeds in your mind that will hopefully sprout into eloquent answers when you're bs-ing about what an, um, team player you are.

Dating Etiquette

1. The check. Pony up and pay, cheapskate. You asked her, you pay. If she, in some bizarre reversal of normative gender roles, asked you, you still pay. Yes, even if she insists. Von Sperling didn't recommend it, but if the young lady is too insistent, wave a switchblade at her and say, "Don't think I won't, bitch!"

2. Taxicab. Open the door for her, close it, then walk around the cab and get in on the other side (she shouldn't have to sidle over on the seat to make room for you, or so the argument goes). Bonus points if you refrain from getting dummied by oncoming traffic on the walk around.

3. At dinner. If you want to order a bottle of wine, but aren't entirely sure how to pronounce said bottle/don't want to admit to your date that you're ordering the cheapest bottle on the menu, here's an easy trick: Hold up the wine menu, point to the desired bottle, and tell the waiter, "I'll have this one, please." If she asks, simply smile and say, "Oh, one of my favorites. It's a surprise." Don't tell her the surprise is that you ordered the cheapest bottle of wine.

4. When she gets up, stand up. When she comes back, stand up. Unless she's playing a fake-out game, in which case, double pump fake, then take it up strong. You'll get the basket and the foul. "And one, bitch!"

5. The next morning: One-night stand or not, get up before she does, make coffee, and pay for a light breakfast. If it was a one-night stand, she's probably feeling as uncomfortable as you are; rather than ignore her in an attempt to get her out the door as fast as possible (dick), try to partake in at least ten minutes of genial conversation. And don't leave your number unless you actually want her to call. If not, leave her the number of your friend Todd and have him answer the phone, "Oink oink, fatty," for two weeks.

6. Compliments. Avoid the trite ("Your tits are bomb-ass") in favor of those she probably doesn't get on a regular basis. Mentioning that she has nice cheekbones, or great presence or that her scent really goes well with her chemistry are more likely to impress than the ones she gets on a regular basis. Especially if you're dating an organic chemist.

Dinner Etiquette

1. No matter what the situation, it's always better to come overdressed than underdressed.

2. Basics. Butter plate to your left, glass to your right. Crossing your utensils on your plate is the universal sign for

"pause;" laying your utensils down diagonally and side by side, pointing in the 10-4 position (assuming your plate is a clock), is the universal sign for "done." Wielding your knife in your right hand and your fork in your left and threatening to stab the waiter is the universal sign for "My steak is overcooked, jerkass."

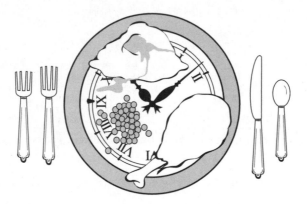

If putting down your utensils pointing to ten and four o'clock is too difficult to conceptualize, replace your plates with clocks. Your dinner guests will just think you are being artsy and not illiterate.

3. Eat slowly. It takes twenty minutes for your brain to register that your stomach is full, which means the more time you take between bites, the less you'll likely eat, and the skinnier you'll stay. This advice is irrelevant if you're eating lard, of course.

4. Know your limits. If your monocle tends to fog up right when you've come in from outdoors, arrive at the restaurant a few minutes early. Check your cane and top hat

at the door, and enjoy a nice port before your date arrives. If your company has been struggling lately, don't use a hundred-dollar bill to wipe your mouth; a fifty will suffice in a pinch. Your date may notice and be impressed that you're slumming it like a regular bohemian.

Now. Don't you feel more European already? No? Then go smoke some cigarettes and bitch about American foreign policy in the Middle East, asshole.

QUICK TIP: Your napkin should always stay in your lap, unless you want to use it to make a 1930s-style bandit mask. Oh, man, those things are hilarious. Then make sure to cover your nose so they can't get a good composite sketch of you while you leave the joint.

Revolving Door Etiquette

There's no bigger dating etiquette conundrum than a revolving door. These rotating monstrosities have caused more in-date nervous breakdowns than uncontrolled flatulence and parallel parking combined. The problem is fairly simple: When you come upon a revolving door, what do you do? Do you go in first to get it moving so it's not so heavy for the young lady? This option seems similar to holding the door open for someone. But then you're going in first and cutting in front of her. Is that rude? Nobody knows . . . not even God himself, which is why He only goes to restaurants with regular doors, mostly Chili's.

The easiest way to unravel this quandary is by scouting your date locales beforehand. Anything that's got a revolving door is off-limits. If you come upon one by surprise, tell your date your appendix just burst, double over in pain, and hope she slowly backs away from your writhing body. The other, more sensible option is to defuse the etiquette awkwardness by drawing attention to it. Just outright say, "Oh, man, I never know what to do about this. Either way I'll look rude! Here, after you." After you throw this one out there, you can do no wrong. Unless you jam your foot right in there as she finds herself halfway between the inside and out, but we don't really suggest that. She won't think you're rude, just honestly confused by the situation. It's only rude if you go first because you're oblivious and selfish. This way is self-deprecating, quirky, and charming. Much like a revolving door itself . . .

Ordering Wine in a Restaurant

Ordering wine in a restaurant, particularly on a date, is a fairly daunting process. Since everything has at least a 400 percent markup on it, you know you're getting ripped off and will be paying around forty bucks for a ten-dollar bottle of shiraz you could have drunk at home. You also don't want to just order the cheapest thing on the menu, because even if it's good, you will look stingy in front of your date. Restaurants know this, and they twist your arm. How to avoid the situation?

The easiest way is to make sure your date doesn't see the wine list and to just order the cheapest thing on the list. Unless she knows about wine or it comes in a plastic jug, she probably won't know it's cheap, and most nice restaurants bring one wine list to the table and give it to the man. Score one for outdated gender roles and run with it.

If the entire wine list is given to both of you, you can still get away with ordering the cheapest bottle if you think ahead. Immediately look at the list and say, "Hmmm . . . how odd . . ." When she asks what seems odd, just point out that the wine list is very odd, and they have a top-flight bottle at the bottom of the price list. Then spout a made-up fact about it, such as, "They must be confused . . . 2003 was a great year, they must have meant it was their 2004, which was kind of one-dimensional." Great, now you don't look cheap, just smarter than the sommelier.

If for some reason your date knows what she's talking about, which can happen if, say, you go out with a winemaker's daughter, you can give up and order beer or cocktails. You can get brave, though, and ask the waitress or sommelier for a recommendation. At this point, you should subtly point to the cheapest bottle on the list. An experienced waiter will pick up on this little tell, and he'll recommend that bottle, probably by saying it's a great value or really underrated. Remember to tip them well for this little help.

Using one of these tactics, you should be able to get out of the dinner without losing your shirt, although it might come off after the second bottle of wine.

When the wine comes, you're faced with a whole new roadblock: the ritualistic opening of the bottle by the waiter. This is an easier process to fake your way through. The waiter will present the bottle so you can see its label. If it's what you ordered, nod approvingly. He will then remove the cork and hand it to you. Unless you want to look like an ass, don't put it to your nose. All that will really tell you is whether it smells like a wine cork. Instead, just inspect it for signs of obvious damage that would ruin the flavor by letting in air. The waiter will then pour an ounce or two of wine into your glass for you to taste. You're looking for signs of spoilage, oxidation, or bacterial infection. Don't worry if you've never tasted a tainted wine before; you will immediately know if you get one. Bad wine tastes like damp cardboard or worse, and it will be tough not to spit it out. If it tastes like normal, good wine, nod your head and say something to the effect of "Yum!"* The waiter will then serve everyone, and you can commence getting happy on wine.

If you want to go even cheaper, hand the waiter a note to the sommelier. Your date will think you're an expert who needs to communicate directly with the sommelier. Have it read, "Dude, I'll give you ten bucks if you'll pour some cheap vodka in a pitcher of grape Kool-Aid. What? No? Okay, double or nothing if she doesn't notice." He'll play ball, and you'll save some cash. Oooooh yeah!

QUICK TIP: It's rude to interrupt the waitress on a date and tell her, "We'll just have water, thank you. Tap!" especially if she's taking dinner orders. "Don't worry, baby; the bread here is out of this world."

---

*Your word choice may vary, as this is not a rigid process.

Getting Someone to Reveal His Name

You've been talking to a person for about fifteen minutes now, and he seems to know a lot about you. Unfortunately, you don't even know his name. It seems inconsiderate to follow personal questions by asking, "What's your name?"

"Hey, how's your job going? I hear you got a promotion; that's great!"
"Thanks. What's your name?"

Depending on his relationship with you, there are different ways to approach extracting a name from your currently anonymous acquaintance.

Doesn't Look Familiar/He Definitely Knows You

Sometimes you will have no idea how this person even knows you. Under these circumstances it's necessary to employ the introduce-them-to-somebody-else method. Grab somebody you do know and tell that person, "Oh, hey, this is my friend, so-and-so." When they introduce themselves to each other, pay attention. You probably weren't listening the first time he said his name; you have to make sure you do this time.

Looks Familiar/He Definitely Knows You

You know that you know this person; you just don't know how or why. In this situation you can't really introduce him to somebody else because you would have to say his name. Try using the

"Great ID Exchange." Tell them that your driver's license photo is the worst ever, and show it to them. Then ask to see his. Then say, "Okay never mind, yours is the ugliest. Jesus, I had no idea you were this hideous at age sixteen." As you repeat this line from memory, glance at the name. And if you have time, the address. Now you've gone from inconsiderate loser to great friend. "Do you still live at 544 Maple Lane? What? You don't know my address? What kind of one-sided friendship is this!?"

You've Had Sex/She Definitely Knows You

You know how she feels on the inside, but you just don't know what her parents named her. It doesn't seem like that big of a deal, but according to everybody else in society it is. Try to be sly. Ask her how she spells her name. Most names have multiple spellings, but hope to God it's not an easy one. ("Umm . . . J-A-N.") If she asks you why, you can be coy and say, "You'll see . . . ," then walk away. Sure, she'll expect a personalized gift of sorts very soon, or at least a letter, but she also expected you to know her name. Oh-for-two ain't bad!

Takeaway Point: If you don't know somebody's name, be clever. Get it out of him/her, but never guess. "Mike" and "Sarah" may be the odds-on favorites, but still only yield a .03 percent success rate.

Varieties of Wine

Chances are, if you go to buy wine, you're going to be inundated with a flood of names of different varietals and blends, and you really won't have much of an idea what's going on. Here's a quick rundown of what you'll usually find:

Cabernet Sauvignon—Strong red with notes of black currant and other dark fruits. Great with red meats.

Chardonnay—Hearty, popular white often aged in oak to give it a vanilla and other flavors; otherwise has crisp fruity flavor.

Pinot Grigio—Lightly crisp and subtle white that has melon and other fruity flavors and pairs nicely with fish.

Pinot Noir—A lighter red that often has a subtle complexity with cherry or raspberry flavors.

Red Red—Wine you make me feel so fine. Keep me rocking all of the time.

Sauvignon Blanc—Crisp, dry white wine made in Bordeaux.

Shiraz/Syrah—Bold flavors with pepper and chocolate notes, strong enough to stand up to spicy foods.

Heinz 57—Oh, actually, that's not wine. "Sir, will you please take that ketchup bottle out of your ice bucket; it's against restaurant policy."

Pairing Wine with Food

There are obviously lots of exceptions to these rules that snooty know-it-alls will tell you about, so don't say them out loud, but when you're pairing wine with food, it's tough to go wrong with a simple rule. For light foods like fish, chicken, and white meats, you generally can't go too wrong with a chilled white wine. For beef, other red meat, and things like pizza or barbecue, go with a red. This is a gross oversimplification, but it will work in 99 percent of situations. Think of it like this: whites are generally a little more subtle and delicate, so pair them with similar foods. Reds are generally a little heartier, so they can stand up to spices and big flavors a bit better. And as for greens, that's not wine. That's olive oil. It goes well with breads.

Although certain foods go great with certain wines, you shouldn't be a snob about it. For example, nobody needs to know about a fantastic merlot you discovered that complements churros very well. You shouldn't be drinking at a carnival, anyway.

Having a Signature Drink

Despite what a talking animatronic animal may have told you during a Super Bowl ad, you're not going to impress anyone by sidling up to a bar and ordering a Bud Light. Same goes for a Jack and Coke, gin and tonic, and Hershey's chocolate syrup and milk. Instead, try switching it up and being a little more creative with a signature drink of your own. This strategy will help you stand out when everyone else is getting "totally hammered" by ordering shots of Cuervo.

A few ground rules to remember:

- Nothing too complicated. Sure, you can order something with seven ingredients, but it's a pain in the ass for bartenders, takes forever to make, and slows down service for everyone else.

- Make sure it's common enough that bartenders will know how to make it. Nothing's more annoying than having to explain exactly what's in your drink every time you order, then screaming, "I said TEDDY Roosevelt, not FRANKLIN Roosevelt! Did you go to a bartending community college?"

- Pick a drink that may be very difficult to take at first, then grow gradually desensitized to it. That way when somebody else takes a sip and winces, just take a big swig, stare at him solemnly and ask, "What's wrong? Can't handle a little Drano, pussy?"

Some good examples:

> The Manhattan—bourbon, sweet vermouth, a cherry
> The Sidecar—brandy or cognac, Cointreau or triple sec, lime or lemon juice
> The White Russian—vodka, Kahlúa, light cream

SPECIAL TIP: Try having a signature snack as well. Everybody loves a person who can dig into his pockets and take out a single KitKat bar when asked.

Cocktail Vocabulary

Ordering a drink at a bar can be intimidating because unless your parents had serious drinking problems, you didn't grow up using any of the lingo. It's not all that hard, though; here are the key words you have to know:

> Dirty—A drink, generally a martini, in which the brine from the cocktail olives is added.
> Dry—A drink made with dry vermouth.
> Neat—Served "straight": without any mixer or dilution.
> Perfect—A drink with equal parts sweet and dry vermouth.
> Rocks—Served over ice.
> Twist—The outer skin of a fruit is twisted over the glass, releasing oils into the drink.
> Up—A drink served in a stemmed cocktail glass rather than "down" on the rocks.
> Beefy—A glass is filled with five hamburger patties and then a drink is poured on top. (Not recommended.)

Identifying a Bad Bar

There are bars you go to during college, and there are bars you go to after graduating. There's a simple reason: The vast majority of college bars suck. Either you wanted to punch every meathead channeling his inner Bon Jovi during a tone-deaf rendition of "Livin' on a Prayer," or you were that tone-deaf meathead, in which case—FYI—lots of people wanted to punch you. Either/or, it's time for a change.

Of course, as anyone who has been sandwiched between three douche-bag i-bankers discussing who they plan on date-raping over six-dollar Heinekens knows, many real-world watering holes are just as abhorrent as their undergrad counterparts. Luckily, doing a little recon work on the particulars of an establishment allows you to separate the good from the God-awful. Below, signs that you should probably look for an alternate place to imbibe:

Bad Sign #1: People Behaving Like They're Still in College. Drinking that results in the loss of bladder control, the involuntary expulsion of the contents of your stomach, blacking out, incomprehensible babble, harassing fellow bar patrons, and other antisocial behavior is accepted—nay, expected!—in college. Approach that stage of inebriation one too many times after you graduate, though, and you'll become "That Guy." Don't become That Guy. No one likes That Guy. It's imperative, then, that you avoid bars full of Those Guys.

Bad Sign #2: Really Bad Music. Tricky, and by no means definitive, as irony and personal taste make it difficult to universally agree on what's good and what's bad. That said, if some intoxicated female spills her drink on you while gyrating wildly to "Girls Just Wanna Have Fun," and you say to yourself, "If the next song is as shitty as this one, I'm out," and the next song is either "Sweet Home Alabama," "I Love Rock N' Roll," or anything that can be even tangentially categorized as Jersey rock, then you should probably act on your fun fatwa.

Bad Sign #3: The Presence of Golden Tee. It's not so much the game itself, but rather what playing it in a social setting says about you. Namely, "Hi, I play video games in bars because I lack the conversational and cognitive skills required to communicate with members of the opposite sex. I drink too much beer and refer to girls who won't talk to me as 'dumb sluts.' Non-roofie-facilitated sexual encounters of mine in the past six months: zero. I give off an air of faux confidence when I'm drinking pitchers with my bros, but I'm really dying on the inside."

Buying the First Round

Often when you go out with a group of people, you'll alternate buying rounds of drinks. This system makes paying easier, but it's also inherently inefficient. Why should you have to pay for someone else's twelve-dollar cocktail when it's your round if you've been drinking beers all night? That's not very equitable, but if you bring it up, you'll sound like a cheap-skate. Nobody likes any sort of skate, but the general consensus is that cheap ones are the worst. To beat the system, it is of utmost importance that you get there early and buy the first round. For one, it makes you seem like the gentleman because you're getting everybody's first drinks when they are the most

Arriving before your friends and buying yourself a drink isn't considered "getting the first round." Your "friends" aren't coming, are they?

sober to appreciate it. Second, and more important, more people will start arriving later and each round will be that much more expensive. Do you want to be the gentleman who got the first round of four drinks, or the asshole who waited until the last round and bought ten? You may be completely drunk by then but the math is simple: Get the first round.

Doing Shots

Unfortunately, after college, you can't do shots anymore. That's just a rule. You're not drinking just to get drunk as quickly as possible anymore, and that's pretty much all shots are good for. If you're ordering shots, you might as well put on a pair of Underoos and a Little League jersey, because you're saying, "I never grew up." This rule also holds for Long Island iced tea, which is pretty much just an enormous shot.

Restaurant Etiquette

Your normal manners will work fine when you're eating at a Wendy's, Denny's, or anywhere else ending with y's but when you go to a fancy restaurant, it's time to break out what you learned in those etiquette classes. What? You didn't take etiquette classes? Shit, this is bad. This is real bad. Okay, okay . . . calm down . . . we'll figure out something. Just breathe. We're going to get you through this.

The most important thing to remember about table manners in a fancy setting is that they're mostly a combination of rules you already follow plus common courtesy. Some parts are tricky, but for the most part, it's a pretty straightforward system. Continue not chewing with your mouth open. Say please and thank you. On top of that, remember these little tricks to seem really dignified:

- If you answer your phone at the table, you should be forced to eat at IHOP for the rest of your life. This includes texts and anything Blackberry/Treo/Q-related. You can wait until after dinner, you self-important, digital-leashed jerk.

- General rules: Smaller fork is for salad; small spoon over your plate is for dessert. Anything fancier than that should be explained by the waitstaff or brought out with the individual dish.

- Make a reservation well in advance, and if the restaurant doesn't call to confirm the day before you're supposed to eat, take matters into your own hands. Nothing's more embarrassing than taking a date to a place that's lost your reservation. Well, maybe if you got an obvious boner while being told they'd lost it, but that probably won't happen. Unless you have an inconvenience fetish.

- The girl will always offer to pay her share. When she does, wave your hand and go, "No, please." If she continues to protest, look her dead in the eye and say, "Bitch, I will slit your throat with this butter spreader if you don't drop this fucking charade right now." She'll let you pay. What a gentleman!

- The adage that you can tell if someone's nice by how he treats waiters is beyond clichéd. However, if you pay with a credit card, your date *will* sneak a look at the tip you leave, so even if you've been superpleasant with the waiter, you're going to lose points if you leave 10 percent. And "I thought that was twenty percent" isn't a very good excuse, because now you're bad at math in addition to being a jerk.

Bribing a Maître d'

Unless you are James Bond, you're not going to be able to walk into a crowded restaurant on a Friday night and get a table by giving the maître d' a handshake with a few rumpled one-dollar bills in it. Also, for the record, if it's only a White Castle, just wait for people sitting at a table to stand up and leave; that's a vagrant, not a maître d'. Slipping into a crowded restaurant and passing even a ten in your palm is going to get you two things: ten dollars poorer and a contemptuous look. One, ten dollars isn't really any money to a guy who's getting tips all the time at a fancy restaurant, and two, they will probably be insulted both at the attempt to bribe and the small size of the greased palm.

Try it a different way, then. If you're eating at a fancy restaurant where reservations can be hard to come by, think ahead. On your way out, introduce yourself to the maître d' and slip him a twenty as a tip, not a bribe, and perhaps your business card. Then, the next time you need a table for a date or a business outing in the near future, you can give the maître d' a call, ask for him by name, and see what he can do for you. Trust us, he'll remember your good etiquette and take care of you.

Note: At a bakery, try palming a cupcake and shaking the bouncer's hand. The frosting will get all over his hand and he'll hook you up with something "real tasty like." Works like a charm.

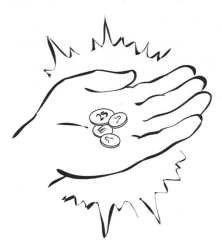

Often times, the maître d' at a fancy restaurant will not share your enthusiasm for loose change, so try bribing him with larger bills.

QUICK TIP: If you're going to use fake Monopoly money on a date, at least use the twenties. They're green.

Getting Called by Name in a Restaurant

Walking into a fancy restaurant and having the maître d' and your waiter call you by name quickly establishes your status as someone who's worth knowing, and it doesn't seem like bragging since you're not doing anything. Your date will be impressed if this happens, but unfortunately, you're not the kind of VIP who warrants this treatment. Still, you can get it if you plan ahead. On the afternoon of your date, go into the restaurant, introduce yourself to the maître d' and if, possible, your waiter. Give them a small tip, something around ten dollars, and explain that you're on an important date and would like to be called by name if they don't mind. Later that night, when you walk in with your date and everyone knows to call you by name, you might as well have them call you Mr. Awesome, because that's what your date will be thinking.

Complaining About Food

Anyone can say, "Wow, this is so good. I love it!" when served a restaurant dish. However, wholehearted approval of everything placed in front of you, be it rack of lamb or soggy Appletiser, really sends a loud message of "When you're eating Easy Mac out of a paper bowl every night, anything's an upgrade." To make it clear you have a refined palate, it's a good idea to make the occasional very specific complaint. This complaint should show that your tongue can parse out the little nuances of an individual ingredient's contribution to the overall dish. Don't come out with something common sense like, "This is salty," or "A bit bland." Swing for the fences with the hope that your dining partner won't know enough to correct you. "Wow, way too much cilantro in this!" or "Cumin is best when used in moderation, but apparently the chef missed that memo." Finally, likening a dish to any of the following is a kiss of death: gas station cappucino, cat food, and Handi-Snacks. (Note: These insults will not work if you're actually drinking a gas station cappucino, or eating cat food and Handi-Snacks.)

QUICK TIP: To seem more important than you are, ask for coffee with milk. When it comes, take a sip, look disgusted and say, "Cow's milk? What am I, a medieval serf?" and throw it across the room.

Funeral Etiquette

Unlike the first three letters of the name, funerals are not fun. They should be called boringerals. But, you guys were best friends for a couple years so you probably should attend—but do you know how to act? Every funeral has an unspoken code of conduct that may sometimes border on counterintuitive. Have no fear, we are here to help. Just follow the rules and you'll get by fine:

Rule 1: We understand this is a very tough time for you. Nobody wants to wake up at 7:00 A.M. on a Saturday, but you cannot be late. It is just plain rude.

Rule 2: No iPod. We don't care if you have a sweet techno remix to "Amazing Grace"; keep your head in the game. People will misinterpret this portable MP3 player as a lack of respect. Is that what you want?

Rule 3: No costumes. It doesn't matter how close the death was to Halloween; you can change into that outfit later. It may seem like no big deal to you, but wearing that murder-scene-from-*Psycho* costume will make you the center of attention at any funeral, when the key here is to blend in as much as possible.

Rule 4: No chanting. When the grieving father goes up to make his eulogy, there is no need to start pounding your feet and yelling, "Speech! Speech! Speech!" He's already going to give a speech. Why do you think he removed that typewritten speech from his breast pocket?

There are many unwritten rules when it comes to funerals. For example, did you know it is considered rude to bring balloons and presents to a friend's burial?

Rule 5: No human carcass marionette. It's not cute, and to keep the illusion the strings would have to be as sturdy as rope but as thin as floss, which is nearly impossible to find. Not worth it.

Bar Mitzvah Etiquette

The average Jew will attend more than 150 bar mitzvahs in his lifetime. The average gentile will attend (a very awkward and foreign) one. Whether it's your girlfriend's little brother or the boss's son, it's important to know how to act during a bar mitzvah so you can get that promotion into a corner office or third base.

You will be around fifty to one hundred thirteen-year-old little Jewish boys and girls, so it's of utmost importance that you watch your mouth. The annoying part is that, at age thirteen, most kids know all of the swear words but their parents still view them as very innocent babies. So when the cool kid (and you better believe there will be a cool kid) tells you to "Go fuck yourself," just smile back at him and tell him to run along and get his caricature done; it's on the house.

At bar mitzvahs, dinner will be served in two shifts: The kids will get a buffet of greasy finger foods, and the adults will get a plate of chicken or fish. As an adult, it is crucial that you don't continually eye the children's buffet while drooling and poking your dry whitefish with a fork. And if you do eye the children's buffet, don't nudge somebody else and motion toward the kids, saying in a sexual voice "Man, I'd love to get me some of that all-you-can-eat action." Bribing a twelve-year-old into giving you fries is okay as long as you two meet at a predetermined rendezvous point outside of the venue. Come alone.

If you never had a bar mitzvah, it's important to know that every party ends by dismantling the decorations, going home, and opening the presents. The presents are usually in the form of checks in envelopes, which are opened by the youngster while an adult records the total, in hopes that it reaches half the cost of the actual party. As each check is read aloud, the family then judges each gift giver by the amount of money received. If you

At most bar mitzvahs it's frowned upon to turn a yarmulke upside down and use it to hold guacamole, salsa, or any dip.

want to seem courteous and knowledgeable give a check for thirty-six dollars. Eighteen is a lucky number in Judaism and so giving twice that is considered very nice and generous. Give thirty-seven dollars, however, and you're nothing but a filthy anti-Semite. Of course, they'd know that anyway when you fell asleep during the entertainment, a rocking set by the Hebrew metal cover band Black Shabbat.

Finally, bar mitzvahs will be a petri dish for fat, ugly, disfigured, and/or disabled preteens. Do your best not to make fun of anyone. You don't know who's related to whom, and it's better to keep all comments nonderogatory. Remember: One man's trash is another man's little cousin.

QUICK TIP: For bat mitzvahs just do the opposite of everything stated above.

Drug Etiquette

When college ends, so should your use of certain drugs. Unfortunately, there's no good way to look like an adult if you're still grinding up Adderall with your student ID so you can snort it. Instead, try your platinum AmEx. Or, better yet, stop snorting crushed pharmaceuticals altogether; the only test you have coming up is an eye exam.

You don't have to give up narcotics completely, but there are subtle ways to class up your usage habits.

- Smoke pot no more than once a week, and don't talk about it. Being a stoner was a perfectly acceptable way to feel part of a subculture and listen to shitty reggae when you were in college, but nobody wants to hang out with an unmotivated pothead who works at an ice cream parlor.

• If you must smoke pot, it's time to buy a bong with some class. Anything shaped like a skull or cartoon character, over a foot long, or made of a milk jug has got to go. Also, if you must name your new bong, don't call it something juvenile like "Stone-a-saurus" or "The Bake-in-ator8000." Instead, go with something that's got an understated dignity, like *The Collected Works of Proust*.

Matching tuxedos for you and your bong provides a great way to seem mature when smoking marijuana.

- Coke is still cool. Not cool: talking about how much coke you do, doing coke by yourself, doing too much coke, looking so tweaked out at 6:00 A.M. that you have to wear sunglasses when you step outside.

- If you're going to tie off to shoot up some heroin, people will be impressed if you pay attention to detail. Don't carry your vials and syringes around in disorganized clumps in your pockets; instead, buy a sharp Euro carrying case. Some friends may call it a "man purse," but they'll secretly respect you. Finding a vein on the first try is more important than ever as you get older, but don't tie off with just any old belt. Your fellow needle-drug users will notice if you've got some Prada or Gucci wrapped around your biceps, and you don't get a second chance to make a first impression like that.

– CHAPTER 10 –

Dating

"Wait a minute. A chapter on dating? Isn't this whole book just a thinly veiled guide to tricking girls into sleeping with me?" Wow, do you always ask this many rhetorical questions as you read? Yes, almost everything else in the book will be at least tangentially useful in your unending quest to get young lovelies to swoon for you, but there are specific maneuvers you can use to fake your way through dating, flirting, or phoning that mail-order-bride company "just for laughs." Oh, wow, they're that cheap? Really? Well, you might as well try one . . .

While most faking requires you to do certain things and act in certain ways, faking it in the dating world requires you avoiding certain situations and refraining from saying certain things. You can't "smack them titties" when you meet her.

Don't say, "Well, your entrée was a few dollars more, so split-ting the check fifty-fifty doesn't seem fair." Don't call eight times the day after your first date, each time saying one letter of "I L-O-V-E Y-O-U" and then hanging up. Yes, these policies seem unreasonable, but if you follow them, you'll look like a classy, aloof guy who knows how to treat a lady without being creepy.

Of course, once you get a young lady to call your very own, the real struggle has only begun. If you think attaining girls is difficult, wait until you try keeping them. A loving committed relationship is very difficult to fake. You'll have to act like you care about every little complaint, and every insignificant quar-rel. "Really? She didn't serve the fruitcake you brought? That Carole has always been trouble, baby. Tell me all about it at halftime."

Finally, it's important not to fake it too well on the first date. Sure, you can show up in a tux and white gloves and remember to chew with your mouth shut for that first outing, and you can maybe even keep it up for the next few dates. However, once you end up in the comfortable rut of a relationship, she's going to find out that your policy on wearing pants is, at best, flexible, and you're going to have to explain why you have a tattoo of Grimace on your chest. (Never, ever make a bet with the Hamburglar; he'll fucking cheat.) This is bound to be a disappointment for her, and she'll accuse you of luring her in under false pretenses. At that point, tell her it's too late; she al-ready signed the marriage papers. She'll claim that those pa-pers are bogus and that you drugged her and put a pen into her hand and wiggled the papers underneath the pen in the shape of her signature. Ha. I'd like to see that hold up in court, sweetie.

You're golden.

Picking Up Young Ladies

Bars and clubs are great for meeting girls, but sometimes they're more effort than they're worth. On top of having to pay for shit, you have to deal with other dudes, loud music, and girls nights out. That's why approaching girls in other public forums is a solid move. If you do it noncreepily, girls will be flattered that you put yourself out there. They also believe in shit like fate and may interpret your calculated run-in in the produce aisle as a sign of divine intervention. Whatever, you need all the help you can get. Over the course of a weekend, we tried picking up girls everywhere from the post office to the park. Here are the best three:

Art Museums

Museums tend to be full of cute art-school brunettes with Elvis Costello glasses and tattoos on the inside of their wrists (the hipster's very own Tramp Stamp) whose view of "women's empowerment" entails sleeping with every unshaven guy wearing Chucks and a Minor Threat T-shirt. Fish in a barrel, right? Eh. Two problems: For one, these girls are usually at the museum with boys they're dating, boys who are trying to date them by appearing cultured, or less attractive (read: fat) female friends. Those who are there alone are usually walking around with those guided tour headphones, thus preventing them from hearing the passage on cubism you memorized from your Art History 101 textbook for precisely this occasion. Second, the line between appearing as an informed, interested museumgoer and a cliché jackass who is there just to pick up chicks is a fine one. It's not hard to bullshit about art—just like on an English essay, you can never really be wrong if you throw in a bunch of multisyllabic words like *canonical*—but you'll be quickly exposed if you're talking to someone who knows her shit. This is why the best place to meet girls in an art museum is . . . the art museum coffee shop. You can accurately assess who she's there with without having to wonder whether her boyfriend is looking at painting in a different wing. You can talk and joke freely without having to worry about being reprimanded by the museum ushers. Finally, and perhaps most important, you don't even have to talk about art if you don't want to. As usual, we found that playing dumb/making jokes was more effective than acting like a know-it-all. If you're with a friend, ask a girl to mediate a debate you're having over (insert name of exhibit here). If you go up to a girl who's looking at a painting and say something along the lines of "This Picasso's okay, but I find it a tad derivative of my earlier work" and she doesn't laugh, well, you picked the one square in the entire museum, so try again.

Clothing Stores

Where are all the pretty girls? In stores, you dick! If you can persuade a good girl friend of yours to take you shopping, you're golden. You can't hang out alone by the women's dressing room without looking like a sketchy pervert, but if you're with a girl (and you're not actually in the changing area), it's way less creepy. Wait for a girl to try on something and when she comes out to look at herself in the mirror, say something gay like, "Oooh, those jeans fit really well," or "I like that dress, but the back is a little weird." Nine times out of ten she'll say, "Really?," after which you say, "Yeah, I think my ex (so she knows your not a 'mo) had something a little less flow-y (or whatever, it doesn't matter), maybe try that?" And she'll be all "Thanks!" Then just keep talking till your actual friend comes over and proves that you're not some loony tune hanging out in the women's department. She'll be impressed that you actually went shopping with a female friend of yours, but make a joke like, "Yeah, we're actually going to an underground dogfight after this," so she doesn't think you're a total metrosexual. Another good intro: When you're standing next to a girl who is perusing a rack, pick up a dress and say, "Do you think this will slenderize my legs?" Guaranteed laugh.

Organic Food Markets

Consider the markup on $6.99-a-pound organic arugula a tax for the privilege of shopping in a literal and figurative meat market. Places like Whole Foods are crawling with girls who think regular supermarkets are for poor people. These are also the sort of girls who refuse to drink tap water and sit around with their friends trying to figure out which character from *Sex and the City* they'd be, but they're usually hot, so what can you do. Ask a girl to help you choose appropriately ripe fruit ("How the hell are you supposed to tell if this papaya is ripe or not?"); better yet, tell her you're cooking dinner for a group of friends

tonight and does she have any suggestions for a good appe-
tizer? The key is just coming off natural and goofy—like you're
not actively trying to hit on her, even though you both know
you are.

QUICK TIP: "Can I buy you a drink?" isn't a suave pickup line
when you are just planning on taking a Coke can out of your
pocket and following it up with "I hope you like caffeine-
free!"

Hitting on a Girl over E-mail

For the great bulk of us, it is almost impossible to look a girl in
the eye and ask her out on a date. When her breasts aren't dis-
tracting us, the overwhelming urge to stare at the ground is. As
recently as 1989, this would have been a crippling problem.
Now, however, cowards can hide behind e-mail to do their flirting. No stammers, no stutters, and no ludicrous sweating problems, just clever, spontaneous banter that you can spend hours
editing and perfecting before hitting "send."

The problem is, girls know that it's just the cowards who are
resorting to this measure, so you really have to elevate your
game. A single flaw could completely derail weeks of carefully
crafted wordplay. Here's how you make it happen.

The first e-mail you send has to be playful and nonthreatening. Make some jokes and ask some questions so she has something to respond to. Don't make any plans yet or allude to any
intentions. Your ultimate goal may be getting a date, but the
first e-mail is just to gauge how possible it is.

First E-mail Do's

"Hey, it was fun talking with you on Saturday. I sincerely hope I smelled appropriately."

"Beth gave me your contact info. Don't worry; she only told me the first six digits of your Social Security number. She's a stickler for privacy, isn't she?"

First E-mail Don'ts

"I want to see you again. Soon."

"Shaking your hand when I left broke my heart. I hoped we would hug. The kind of hug where the two people rub each others' backs in a circular motion."

If you get a timely and favorable response to e-mail number one, it's time to step up one intimacy level. Ask what she is doing later this week. Don't suggest anything yet, just merely inquire if she is free. And leave her open to suggest time/place.

Second E-mail Do's

"Would you be free next week to hang out in person? I've got some great jokes that I wouldn't dare type out (it's all in the vocal delivery)."

"Hey, we should meet up some time; my typing skills will only impress you so much."

Second E-mail Don'ts

"You. Me. Four bottles of wine. I already made the reservations. Get your coat."

"I'm sending this e-mail from outside your place. The wire-
less reception is great. So is that shirt you're wearing."

If she says she is free and available, then you're almost there.
The second e-mail hump is the hardest to get over, but if she is
free to hang out, then suggest something. Nothing too fancy or
ridiculous; just a meeting for the two of you. If she's made it
this far, it's hard to say no now.

Third E-mail Do's

- "I actually know this really good restaurant opening up if
  you're interested. If not, I make a killer Boboli pizza. The
  secret ingredient is cheese."
- "I don't suppose you like food, do you? I'm absolutely mad
  for it. I can eat up to three meals a day if left unchecked.
  Hopefully we can eat one together?"

Third E-mail Don'ts

- "I'm supposed to go home this weekend; it's my parents' anniversary. I would love for you to be my date."
- "I have two one-way tickets to Delaware. Dover is lovely this
  time of year, so won't you join me on an indefinite vacation? Your boss already told me he'd give you the time
  off."

Note: At this point you will have to physically talk to her, but
most of the legwork is done. Don't bring your laptop to the
date; she won't be checking her e-mail when she's actually
with you.

When hitting on a girl over e-mail, it's important that you don't
hide in a bush by her house. Instead, do it from the comfort of your
own home.

Hitting on a Girl on a Plane

Minutes before boarding a flight, most men will sit down at
their gate and scan the waiting area for any unbelievably attractive women that may be forced to sit next to them for several
hours. If you are lucky enough to find one, you anxiously board
your plane and wait for her to walk down the aisle, hoping to
God she pauses at your row and says, "Oh, can I squeeze by?"

Unfortunately, this rarely happens.

But what happens when it does? How do you react when you win this airborne lottery? This opportunity only presents itself to even the most frequent of fliers once in their lifetime, so you'd better take advantage of it.

Whatever you do, don't talk to her before the plane takes off. Remember, this may be a one-flight-in-a-million chance for you, but to her, she's always the hot girl sitting next to some guy. If you hit on her before takeoff, she'll be annoyed at you the whole flight. If you don't even look at her before takeoff, she'll let her guard down. She'll start to doubt her own beauty and why you're not hitting on her. She'll get desperate. Maybe even desperate enough to order some of those antiwrinkle skin creams from *Sky-Mall* since she'll get free shipping on any order placed in-flight.

After takeoff, say something light, playful, intelligent, and modest. "You know, those lavatories have just enough space for me to push your shit in" doesn't really come off very suave. Instead, make a comment about a book or tabloid magazine she's reading. "I bet fifty percent of this magazine's sales come from people needing something to read on an airplane" or "You know, they shouldn't call it *Us Weekly;* I'm barely even in this issue." Remember, regardless of what you say, she'll respond with "What?" because the din of the airplane is always louder than you think, and if you yell at her off the bat, it may creep her out. She may not be able to hear you because her ears have popped, but it's important not to to pinch her nose and tell her to blow as hard as she can. That's really more of a second-date thing.

If she's not responding, or if she puts on that satin eye mask that helps her sleep, it's probably best not to keep talking to her. For one, she probably doesn't want to speak to you anymore, and for two, she probably has some major ocular issues that you don't want to deal with in the future. Seriously, whose eyelids are so thin that they don't shield enough light!? You don't want to claim any baggage like that until the flight is over.

Just as a warning, it's very possible that the lady you're hitting on is a fifteen-year-old in disguise. Women are developing breasts and Travelocity accounts earlier than ever these days. One tactful way of asking her how old she is is to smoothly bring up emergency-row seating into conversation. "Are you at least sixteen, and would you be able to sit there and assist other passengers in the case of an emergency?" It may seem a little forced, but you don't want to get off the plane and have her daddy waiting at the gate to kick your ass. If she's sixteen, it's still technically illegal but easier to rationalize to your mom when you make that one call from jail.

In conclusion: The hot girl on the plane is one of our greatest flying myths, right up there with Santa Claus and FDR wearing a jetpack. However, if you get lucky and aren't too aggressive, you can get her phone number before you part ways to make your connecting flights. It doesn't matter that she lives in Seattle and you live in Akron. You'll always have the tiny cups of ginger ale you shared from the in-flight drink service, and nobody's going to take those away.

Building an Online Networking Profile

At some point, you'll tire of being rejected by women made of flesh and blood and will decide to move on to ones made of electrons and pixels. This goal will either be achieved by playing much more Leisure Suit Larry or by signing up with a social networking site like MySpace. Now, you may think the bulk of your work is done when you swallowed your pride and signed up for the site, but you're immediately forced to come up with a clever and witty profile to lure people in. You wouldn't go fishing without bait, would you? Well, then why would you sign up for this outdoor-life message board without knowing your favorite kinds of bait. Avoid these common pitfalls:

- Most sites will ask you what you're "Here for." Even if you are most certainly there for dating, you should only check "Friends." Admitting that you're there for dating will completely blow your cover and make you look like some sort of pathetic lothario. Also, if a woman sees the "Dating" box checked, she translates it as "Here for: Finger-banging." That's a tough sell.

- When it asks for your income, don't answer. This is just impolite in proper company. If you make a lot of money, it will sound like bragging and no one will believe you. If you don't make any money, ha ha, you're poor! Nobody wants to befriend someone who made nineteen dollars selling handicrafts last year. Nice God's eye, though; that yarn combination is really sweet.

- Don't list anything by John Grisham as your favorite book. People will think you're semiliterate. Yeah, everyone reads and enjoys them, but no one's going to make the argument that they are great pieces of literature. Instead, try a long book that no one ever finishes, but everyone knows is long. Since no one's ever finished *The Brothers Karamazov,* no one will be able to ask you any prying questions about the ending. You're golden.

- When sending unsolicited messages to strangers, it's important to make it seem like you're genuinely interested in something in their profile other than their picture. While it may seem like anyone would be flattered to receive a message that begins with "Damn girl, that is some ass! . . ." they'll probably stop reading before they get to your analysis of their artistic and literary tastes. Instead, use Wikipedia to learn one interesting fact about something they list as a favorite, and ask if that knowledge affects their enjoyment.

- If somebody leaves you an incriminating message on your profile page, you may want to delete it. Comments such as, "Remember last night?! Oh, man, that nun didn't even see it coming!" may affect what people think about you.

- Lastly, when choosing a picture for your profile, don't pick something that shows off your barbed-wire tattoo. Trust us on this one.

Quirky Dates

You can be cool and confident when you ask a girl out, but if you really want her to think you're a cut above, you've got to deliver some sort of awesome, mind-blowing activity for the big night. Dinner dates are therefore out of the question unless you're willing to spend some serious coin to take her to a superfancy place she wouldn't be able to go to otherwise. At the same time, though, if it's too fancy, you'll seem like you're trying too hard. Now you've got to find something quirky and offbeat that will seem like you're an interesting, creative guy who came up with this on his own. Something like:

- Volunteering. This one is truly the antifancy restaurant. Say something like, "We could go out to some fancy dinner, and that would be fun. I just feel like we'd get to know each other better by working on this Habitat for Humanity house for an afternoon." This date has several strengths. First, it's free. Second, you'll seem like you have a social conscience. Finally, in some jurisdictions you get to count the hours of anyone else you recruit against your community-service debt. Only 196 hours to go and that public intoxication is off your record! You're gettin' laid tonight!

- Academic lecture. Going to a reading or lecture by a famous thinker further establishes you as someone who's smart and in-the-know. However, you're not that smart, so it doesn't matter what topic you pick. Anything that sounds reasonably interesting works, and usually they have free little cups of white wine afterward. You'll learn something, spend no money, look classy, and get tipsy. You're gettin' laid tonight!

- Your mother's funeral visitation. It's a hard time for you to be charming, but you're already going to be dressed up and your entire extended family's going to be there. You might as well bring some impressive arm candy along for the ride, just to squelch those rumors about you being a loser. To earn extra points for sensitivity, break down crying when you look in the casket and say, "She looks just like herself . . . they did such a good job with the makeup. . . ." You're gettin' laid tonight!

QUICK TIP: It's fine to show a date your collection of comics, but they'd better be in near-mint condition at the very least. She may be accepting, but she can't tolerate seeing Ghost Rider get abused like that.

Lying About What You've Been Arrested For

Maybe you've never committed so much as a jaywalking violation, which is very helpful when filling out the Have-you-ever-been-convicted-of-any-felony?-If-so-explain box on job applications. Unfortunately, that's not going to impress the kind of potential friends, particularly potential mates, who are looking for someone with some ragged edges. Inventing a fictitious story about your "first arrest" for something relatively minor can give your cred a huge shot in the arm. Now, how to pull off this tricky maneuver?

First, remember not to make up any sort of serious violation. It's one thing to be edgy, but it's something entirely different to have spent eight years in a Pyongyang prison cell for heroin trafficking. Other things you can get off pretty easily for, like consensual statutory rape, will leave a similarly bad taste in people's mouths. Instead, try something simple. Speeding at a level that mandated an overnight stay in jail, underage public intoxication, or punching a cop in the face for being a "total fucking asshole" are all acceptable.

Once you've settled on an offense, you need to get your story straight. The exact context of the event itself isn't important; people are going to want to hear about how you actually went to jail. Remember to keep saying, "Look at me! I was scared shitless to be going to jail. When they took my mug shot, that's when it hit home for me." Talk about how the ink from the fingerprinting wouldn't come off your fingertips for days. Describe the holding cell you were in, and talk about how you made friends with dudes who were there for not paying their child support or for kidnapping a hooker. Don't forget, your listener is going to want specifics, so make up some good ones. Don't have yourself staying in jail too long, but say it was "the scariest six hours of your life." Of course, when it went to court, you totally got off because the charges were bullshit, but you've seen the inside of the joint. The clink. Ol' pokey. People will quietly respect you, and women will love your bad-boy flair.

Seeming Religious Enough in a Pinch

Sometimes you may find yourself at a party or on a date and things are actually going well. You are shocked at how well the conversation is flowing and how interested you two are in each other; it seems too good to be true. Then she has to go ahead and ruin it with a line like "Yeah well, I can't stay up too late. I've got to go to church in the morning!"

Background music slows down to a halt and you suddenly become acutely aware of the beads of sweat on your forehead.

While your first inclination is to say something like, "What, is that part of your probation or something?" you should know that these things are important to some people. You might think this means you won't be having sex on the first date, but that's not true, either. Lots of these self-righteous types are superslutty, so just wait it out. You're going to need to be morally flexible to be disingenuous about something as sacred as religion, but if you've made it this far in the book, it's probably not a big issue.

At your age, even most people who consider themselves religious, no matter what religion it is, have pretty much lapsed and stopped going to church, temple, or whatever. This fact means that you don't have to have any truly active displays to be religious in your own eyes and, more important, the eyes of your mate. Instead, you can just fake your way through seeming religious. Here's the gist of it:

- Nothing is easier than acting Christian. If you're a white gentile, everyone will automatically expect you're Christian if you're any religion at all. Steer clear of Catholicism, which has all sorts of rituals you'll be expected to know about, and claim some low-impact Protestant denomination like Methodism or Lutheranism. Basically, all you need to remember here is Jesus. Pretty good dude, and 100 percent magical. A good way to keep track of Christian fundamentals is: if it's courteous or kind to someone else who isn't gay, you're in the clear. Jesus pretty much wanted everyone to be nice to one another, so it's not rocket science to stick with His dogma.

- Judaism is a bit tougher, but it's also more obvious when it's going to be a problem. Anyone who's really serious about her religion won't go out with you if you're not Jewish, so you don't have to worry about it being sprung on you middate. However, if you're already a Jew, but not very observant, you may be squashed. If she starts to bring up more and more conservative beliefs, pat the top of your head. Pat it again, frantically. Stand up and say, "Where's my yarmulke? Did someone steal it? Oy vey, this is bad! We hafta go. Like, now," and run to your local yarmulkery. Don't get the smiley-face one; it looks juvenile. Go with a nice flat black instead, and don't forget the barrettes to clip it to your hair. Phew. Crisis averted.

- If the girl is Neopagan, don't you dare touch that salt shaker. It is her creator god, and she will not put out for that kind of disrespect.

- Anything beyond this and you're on your own. You might want to consider taking the universal escape hatch of "I feel that organized religion is an oppressive force used to keep the privileged in power." This is Marx's argument, not yours, but even most coffee-shop Communists

haven't read all of *Das Kapital,* so you're fine with it. You
don't want to seem completely nihilistic, though, so follow it up with: "But I am very spiritual and believe in a
Judeo-Christian God who is the Creator and a benevolent
force in the universe." Ah, you've covered all your bases
there.

Seeming more religious oftentimes calls for subtlety, so refrain
from baptizing your date in her soup.

QUICK TIP: On a date, point to the shiniest star and tell her
that it's Mercury. This won't work if it's a glow-in-the-dark
sticker on your ceiling, though.

My Date Died! What to Do?

If you go on many dates, odds are one of them will die when you are with her. Choking, car accident, homicide—it's all fair game. The most important preparation is to expect the unexpected. However, exactly how you deal with your dead date will ultimately be predicated upon how long you've been seeing the person. (Note: While the following actions are considered polite in many social circles, the specific rules change from region to region, so take these suggestions as guidelines rather than strict rules.)

First date: The first-date death shouldn't affect you in the slightest. You were just getting to know the person, so there isn't any real sense of loss on your end. Excuse yourself from the table and walk away. If anybody asks you how it went, say she was a real bore and deathly afraid of normal conversation. It's like lying and telling the truth at the same time!

Dating one–six months: You guys are starting to get pretty serious, but her death shouldn't be anything you need to react to. Dates will still be fairly casual (carnival, movie, drinks), so if tragedy strikes try not to make a big deal of things. Walk away and make an anonymous phone call to 911. They can't track your cell phone number if you enable caller ID block (*67 on most phones.) Just calmly tell them the address of the deceased, and go get yourself a frozen yogurt to unwind.

Dating six months–two years: Uh-oh. Things were starting

to get serious, then she up and died on you. If she dies on a serious date like a weekend vacation or trip, you are going to have to call her family and tell them the bad news. Try to remain upbeat and preface it with something light-

There are many awkward intricacies when it comes to dating. However, a mate dying on you middinner does not have to be one of them.

hearted: "You guys are totally gonna hate me, but . . ." It should be a rough two weeks, but at least you're still alive.

Two–five years: This is a stickier situation because odds are you guys were living together and contemplating marriage. Death can strike anywhere at this point, even in your bed. The most annoying part is that most people are going to blame you. But that's the risk you take when you nickname yourself "Natural Causes." At this point, you are beyond just excusing yourself from the table or being the bearer of bad news, you are well into funeral-planning mode. Tell her parents you'll take care of the hors d'oeuvres if they get "all that other stuff taken care of." It seems like a fifty-fifty responsibility split, but all you gotta do is get one of those hundred packs of pigs in the blanket. Suckers.

Fancy Dates on a Tight Budget

$160 may seem like a lot of money to spend on a fancy dinner date, but as long as you can keep the rest of your week's food budget under $50, you're still at a respectable $30-a-day average for food. Living for six days while only spending $50 on food is tough, especially if you have a job and eat lunch out every day, but it's not impossible.

1. No Breakfast—Sorry, but if you're going to take your lady out to a nice-looking restaurant, you'll have to start by cutting Froot Loops out of your diet for the next week.

No breakfast may be tough, but it's a great way to slice your weekly meal requirements from twenty-one to a more manageable fourteen. If you get hungry before lunch, have a glass of water or steal a bagel from a coworker. He'll never see it coming.

2. Sandwiches, Sandwiches, Sandwiches—In terms of bang for your buck, no lunch is more efficiently affordable than sandwiches. For about twenty dollars you can get a loaf of bread, some of your favorite cold cuts, and all of your favorite fixin's for the week. If you're feeling particularly frisky, spend an additional five dollars on side chips for the week. You should have about twenty-five dollars for the six dinners you have left.

3. Pastafarian—If you think sandwiches are an inexpensive form of filling yourself up (and you should be, based on the convincing argument we just made), then wait till you eat pasta. Most spaghettis cost about sixty-nine cents a package, with each package containing enough pasta to fill you up for three dinners. Purchase about five of those for three dollars and spend another ten dollars on sauce and precooked meatballs and/or veggies. You'll get about five dinners out of this method for thirteen dollars, leaving you twelve dollars for one last normal meal out—a pasta break—before the big date.

Eating sandwiches and spaghetti for a week may seem like a horrible way to live, but when she sees that you're spending $160 on marmalade-braised duck, sea urchin ceviche, and wine for dinner she won't have the slightest clue that you're really just jonesing for a fat bowl of Cocoa Puffs.

Seeming Sensitive on a Date

So you're not that sensitive. You laughed when Bambi's mother got shot, and you once looked for the *Schindler's List* DVD in the comedy section. ("It should be right here next to *The School of Rock!*") Unfortunately, that kind of callousness isn't going to win you the affections of any young ladies. Instead, you need to seem sensitive, thoughtful, and considerate. For people who actually have these qualities, they run all the way down to the soul of their beings. For the rest of us, the illusion isn't too difficult.

The first thing to remember is that girls often confuse "sensitive" with "not self-absorbed." Achieve this effect by not talking about yourself, no matter how much you want to. Compound it by asking repeated questions about her. Anything goes: her childhood, her job, her favorite things . . . people like talking about themselves. Go with it. You'll already seem like a prince of a fellow who's not completely in love with himself. If she can answer any questions about your life following the date, you've blown it.

You can gain even more traction by occasionally interjecting seemingly sensitive comments into her stories, which will inevitably turn sad and depressing. "Oh, that's terrible. No dog owner wants to outlive their pet," can turn some boring story about how her dog got hit by a car when she was eight into a guaranteed chance at second base. Keep plumbing the depths of her childhood trauma. It will make her insecure and vulnerable to an attack from the MakeOut Monster, aka you.

Defusing the Emergency Call

Most guys don't know it, but when a girl goes on a first date with a young man she doesn't know all that well, or is particularly nervous about seeing, she'll have one of her girlfriends place an "emergency call" to her in the middle of the date. If the date is going poorly, she'll answer and then explain to the guy that she's really sorry, but her friend is having an emergency of some sort, and she has to rush to her pal's aid. Such a gesture would be very noble if it weren't total bullshit. If she doesn't like you, fine, but she should at least have the chutzpah to come right out and say it. Don't slink away to console some friend whose hypothetical boyfriend just gave her the imaginary dumping of a virtual lifetime.

So now that you're savvy to this cunning ruse, what can you do about it? While it may seem hopeless at first, you have a couple of options. If the date is really going poorly, you're probably better off just letting her answer the call and playing along to save yourself any additional awkwardness. However, if you think you can turn things around and finish strong, your strategy is clear: As soon as she looks at her phone, jokingly say, "Did you tell one of your friends to call you in case the date was going terribly?" At this point, you've completely retaken the advantage; her plan has been foiled. She was only using such a transparent out because she was too scared to be straight with you, so she's not going to outright say, "Yes, I'm having a bad time." Instead, she'll laugh and not answer the call. Inside, she'll be impressed that you were clever enough to see past her feminine trickery. Outside, this is what's known as holding someone "emotionally hostage." Never mind that, the making out will taste twice as sweet now.

Late-Night Text Messages

There's only one reason to send a text message after 11:00 P.M., and it's not to let someone know that their favorite infomercial is on again. We're not going to fault you for wanting some late-night tail, but you need to be somewhat discreet about it. After all, she's a girl you call, not a call girl.

Don't: Be forward or abrupt. For example, "U up?" shows very little effort, poor grammar, and very little regard for your potential partner. Instead, try, "Hey, are you awake?" Extra letters are a sign of extra respect.

Do: Own a cellular telephone. Nobody wants to get a late-night fax.

Don't: Suggest having sex. Instead, use phrases like "Want to watch a movie?" or "Want to come over?" That way, you can text many of her friends as well, because there's no such thing as a "repeat movie offender" or a "serial watcher."

Do: Customize the message if you feel the need to send to more than one recepient. People can tell that you sent a mass text message when they all say "Hey YOURNAME, just thinkin' about you . . . You still like YOURFA-VORITEMOVIE? I just rented it." This isn't *Wheel of Fortune;* nobody wants to fill in the blanks.

Takeaway Point: When texting for late-night fun, be vague and know when to quit.

Texting is a great passive way to let her know you care, but the subtlety can be ruined in a heartbeat with an inappropriate message.

Secret Crushes and When to End Them

You meet somebody new. There is an attraction there. A spark. A hint of chemistry. For some reason or another you can't do anything about it. She's unavailable. You're too young. She's fictional. You're not drunk. She's your cousin. You're her imaginary friend. The reasons are infinite, but the results are always the same. You are falling secretly in love with this person and she has no idea.

You need to imagine your crush as a fruit fly: Give it a life expectancy of two weeks before crushing it with a swatter and flushing it down the toilet of repression. Crushes that last longer than two weeks begin to linger in loser territory and eventually fully set up shop in Patheticville, USA. While it may seem romantic that you have been crushing over the same girl for five years, it's actually the thing about you that your friends hate the most. Weird, huh?

"What can I do? I can't pretend I don't like her anymore." Actually, that's exactly what you can and should do. First, you need to convince your friends that you are over her, then eventually you will have convinced yourself. If you lie to yourself long enough, it becomes truth. If that doesn't work, get a new crush. Most people are only capable of having one, so once you get a new crush, the old one will be mathematically eliminated. How about that girl from the supermarket cash register? You think she asks *everybody* if they have a club card? Doubtful, stud.

Turning a Friend into a Lover

There are few situations more uncomfortable than falling in love with one of your close friends. Making the transition from boy who is a friend to boyfriend is one of the hardest maneuvers since slicing bread. However, if you are willing to risk your friendship with this lady, you may still have a chance to make the switch from other to significant other.

Step 1: Act uninterested. If you have a crush on your friend, odds are she is attractive. She probably has many other male friends who have a crush on her as well. Girls hate when their friends come on to them, so don't be that guy. Don't be the guy who wants to give her massages or plays with her hair in an eerie fashion; she probably hates it. If you are the only one who plays it cool around her, she'll be naturally more gravitated to hang out with you instead of them.

Step 2: If all is going well, she should be hanging out with you more often. Arrange meetings that seem like dates, but continue acting cool. Rent a DVD or eat dinner together. Never make a move. Don't even hug her hello or good-bye. The sexual tension will mount, but don't give in to temptation. Keep it friendly and be as funny as you can, she needs to become attracted to your personality and physically aloof behavior.

Step 3: After a few weeks, or even months (nobody said this would be easy) of close personal friendship with no physical contact, your relationship should present many opportunities for you to make your move. Sitting close to each other on a couch, staring silently over dinner, bumping hands while walking. Don't pounce on the first one. You need to really make her wonder why you aren't doing anything about it.

Step 4: Make your move. There is no specific rule or instruction for when to make your move, you'll just feel yourself getting nervous and at a certain point you'll subconsciously move in. She won't expect it because you guys have been friends so long without even a hint of any physical interaction. She may even be confused, but ultimately she should feel relieved. Turns out you did like her after all and that you weren't, in fact, gay.

Note: Step 4 may also turn out to be a horrifying experience that ruins your friendship. Either way, it should make for an awesome story.

QUICK TIP: Never take a dare that embarasses you in front of a potential mate. The only exception to that rule is during a "double-dog dare."

Stealing a Girl from a Boyfriend

So you wish that you had Jesse's girl? The bad news is the girl you have a crush on has a boyfriend. The good news is this maneuver, while difficult to accomplish, is not impossible. If you ask your parents how they fell in love, it's not very uncommon for them to say, "Well, I was dating somebody else, but your father stole me away!" Then your parents will share a good laugh as the person who was dating your mom takes their order. How do you turn your crush's boyfriend into a deadbeat waiter? In some ways it's not even as hard as getting a girl without a boyfriend to fall for you. Instead of having to be better than all other guys in the world, you only have to outdo this guy Steve she's been dating since college. Hey, Steve, you have to be employed somewhere initially before you can be between jobs.

Step One: Choose the Right Girl—If your girl is completely and unequivocally in love with her current boyfriend, this isn't going to happen. No matter how nice you are, no matter how many gifts you buy her, no matter how many times you kill her boyfriend, she's not going to leave him.

Step Two: Befriend Her—Guys are often suspicious of their girlfriends' other male friends because they think they all just want to have sex with her. They seem paranoid, but in this instance they're completely completely right. You have to crawl before you can walk, and you have to become her innocuous male companion before you will become her new lover. The more platonic time you spend with her the better—guys get jealous when other straight guys hang out with their girlfriend, girls hate jealous boyfriends, and pretty soon you'll have planted the seeds for tiny fissures that will soon grow into seismic relationship faults.

Step Three: Fill in the Gaps—As her new friend, you have all the juicy details about what her boyfriend doesn't do that she wishes he would. "I don't know. He's a good guy I guess, I just wish he would do nice things for me, like buy me flowers . . ." Note these shortcomings, and then give her what she wants. Don't be ostentatious about it, pick her a single daisy instead of getting her a dozen roses. The nonthreatening nature of your gift will make all the dif-ference.

Step Four: Suggest Nothing—As problems with her current boyfriend begin to snowball, never suggest that they break up—it sounds too suspicious. Instead merely push her in that directions with veiled comments. Use reverse psychol-ogy and plant seeds of doubt in her mind. Then let them blossom into doubt trees that bear delicious rejection fruit. "Sure he's absent-minded and not very ambitious, but who cares right? At least he's kinda good-looking!" You've done your job, and she'll probably dump him.

Step Five: Console Her—If you followed the first four steps precisely enough, within a few weeks you will be ready to console her. Don't rush anything, you haven't gotten this far just to blow it. Take it slow. Make no moves until you're absolutely certain she's okay with it. Then, when you finally do, and she asks you "You didn't try to break me up with my boyfriend because of this, did you?" Just stare into her eyes passionately and lie like you've never lied before.

QUICK TIP: Before you decide to steal a girl from her boyfriend, make sure you want to date her for at least a year. Stealing a girl and then dumping her is not as bad as date rape, but it's close.

Deflecting Beggars on a Date

No matter how witty your anecdotes, no matter how convincing your empathy over the loss of her pet hamster, there's still one thing that can throw a great date off the rails and leave it twisting and writhing in the pain like a fat man regretting one too many Chocodiles before adult lap swim. This malevolent force can only be one thing: an ill-timed panhandling attack.

It usually starts with "Now, I know you folks is out on the

town, but . . ." and ends with you giving the guy a few bucks because you don't want to look like a coldhearted asshole in front of your date. Sounds harmless enough? It's not. It's extortion. They may be homeless, but they're certainly not guileless. They know that there's no way you can save face without giving them at least a few crumpled singles. Congratulations, you've been outsmarted by someone wearing old pillowcases for shoes.

Obviously, you're going to need a delicate touch to defuse this situation without using the word *bum* or resorting to street violence. There are a number of deft feints you can use to get out of this truly horrific situation. Try one of these:

Most dates will not appreciate your usual response of "Get a goddamned job." Instead, you will need to act polite to homeless people who ask for change.

- Say something polite like "Sorry, man, good luck." Then tell your date you saw a *Dateline* special on that guy and that he sells drugs to inner-city youth. She will be impressed with how polite you were and how many television-news-magazine shows you watch.

- Beat him at his own game. Ask him how he liked that sandwich you gave him earlier that day. When he asks what you're talking about, act disgusted that he would take advantage of you like that. Who's the selfish one now? She'll swoon.

- Apologetically say, "Sorry, man, I'm dead broke. You'd know I'd help you out if I could." After he walks away, turn to your date and say, "No, really . . . I'm completely broke. Could I borrow like twenty bucks until payday? I can't go back to the check-cashing place for a few days." She might not be impressed anymore, but, hey, free twenty bucks!

QUICK TIP: It's considered chivalrous to put a jacket on a puddle for a lady to cross, although the effect is considerably undercut if you pull off her jacket and use it.

Acting Sensitive Postsex

Well, you did it. After literally hours of trying, you finally got her to sleep with you. Congratulations, stud, but don't think your work is over. In fact, it's just starting. You see, getting a girl to have sex with you once is the easy part; sealing the deal so you can have sex many more times is considerably tougher. Without some deft maneuvering and suppression of certain urges, that second bang is going to be an uphill climb.

For most men, sex is a flood of emotions, starting with passion, building to satisfaction, and then coming down with "Damn, I'd like to eat half a tray of E. L. Fudges and see how my fantasy baseball team did. Just as soon as I get this condom off . . ." Sure, you can inhale Keeblers and find out that Pujols went to third with two runs scored, but she'll be sitting there resenting you the whole time, thus killing any chance of a double feature. Instead, use the time when everyone's naked and vulnerable to seem like a considerate sensitive guy.

After you take care of business and make your quick run to the bathroom to do some flushing, offer to get her a glass of water. Everyone's sweaty and dehydrated, so this will seem considerate. In point of fact, you just really wanted a glass of water for yourself, but she doesn't have to know that. Quickly return to bed with this small offering, and say the following, no matter how much it hurts you, "Hope you like snuggling!" Did you just vomit a little bit of blood? Yeah, we know, but it's just plain nice to show some affection to someone you've been pursuing. Plus, snuggling is fun; don't act so cool, dude. One caveat, though: If this is some random girl you just picked up in a bar, feel her out on the cuddling issue first, as she may see it as more creepy than endearing. If you do end up spooning, a little extra playing with the hair never hurt, either. Anything that suggests your away message isn't currently "Doggy-style, bi-atch" will really help your cause and make the young lady feel special.

Once you put in a good twenty minutes of totally emasculating cuddling, you're pretty much free to try to initiate a second round of sex. If that doesn't work, immediately give up and return to cuddling for another five or so minutes, then get up and explain that you've got stuff to do. Now is the time to eat cookies and worry about sports, but that last half hour has bought you another round of sex in the future. At the wage you're probably making, this is like trading five dollars for sex, which is a pretty solid deal.

QUICK TIP: Scientists have determined that of all STDs, herpes is the easiest to fake having. Scientists are still not sure why anyone would want to fake having herpes; they're just doing what the research grant told them to do.

Meeting a Girl's Parents

Meeting your young lady's parents is possibly the most nerve-wracking part of dating. It doesn't really have to be, though, since most reasonable parents will yield to their daughter's judgment as long as you don't behave like a complete sociopath. Parents are basically looking for three things: a) that you're polite, b) that you're not potentially violent, and c) that you have some sort of decent career prospects. If you can string this stuff together, they'll probably consent to tolerating you at every other family holiday until they die and leave a disappointingly small inheritance. God, they shouldn't have put so much of their money in pork-belly futures.

No matter what, you can fool them into accepting you. Just follow these steps:

- Be respectful. Give both of them a firm handshake and look them in the eye when meeting them. Don't call them by their first names until they ask you to; stick with "Mr. ____" and "Mrs. ____." Remember to say "please," "thank you," and if you want huge points, "Yes, ma'am." Also, if you're going to their home, don't forget to bring a small gift like a bottle of wine. (A box of wine may be a little more expensive, but it doesn't work as a gesture of appreciation.) If you go over for dinner and want to have her mom love you, offer to help clear the table after the meal.

- Don't voice any opinions. These people realize you're probably banging their daughter, so don't give them any reason to dislike you by voicing any potentially controversial political, religious, or cultural opinions. If the parents are rude and try to directly engage you, chuckle and say, "Well, that's a pretty complex issue. Now, who wants a brownie?"

- Treat this like a date, but with three people. Remember how you got this girl into you in the first place, then extrapolate to her parents. They're normal people, so they'll like talking about themselves. Ask lots of questions, nod in interest, and interject any appropriate wisdom you may have. Otherwise, just keep them talking about themselves. This serves the dual purpose of keeping them from asking prying questions about you while also giving you great personal fodder for . . .

- Your thank-you note. If you go to dinner at her parents' home, you absolutely must write a thank-you note to show your appreciation. Pepper it with personal references like, "I hope your palsy isn't acting up as much today, but I didn't mind when your disobedient limbs flung that bowl of green beans at me!" This shows that you were paying attention and want to establish a deeper connection than a form letter. Keep it polite, but not overly dramatic. Which means no signing it, "Love, your future son-in-law."

Follow these steps and there isn't a sex tape on earth that could surface that would make her parents love you any less. "Oh, you two love-bugs are so cute!"

Defusing a Girl Being Critical of Her Body

Every squirrel finds a nut at some point, so keep on trying your faked lines on young ladies, and eventually it's going to work. You'll end up in bed doing some postcoital snuggling, and you'll compliment some part of her body in an attempt to make her feel nice and possibly win some extra credit. At this point, she will invariably not only fail to take the compliment, she'll throw it back at you by saying, "Oh, God, I hate my (body part). It's my least favorite part!"

Well, you didn't think that far ahead, did you? What, you thought she'd giggle and say thank you? Jesus, no wonder you just lost your virginity on your twenty-seventh birthday; you know *nothing* about women. Now your ass is in a serious crack. You have to successfully deflect this self-criticism, and "Yeah, but that means half of your eyes *aren't* crossed, too!" isn't going to carry any water here. This situation is a sticky one, but you can get out of it with a little planning. Follow these steps:

- You're going to immediately go to hell for doing this, but before giving a compliment, make sure you've pinpointed any problem with her body. This way, you are fully expecting her forthcoming criticism and you can come up with some convincing-sounding counters before you give the initial compliment. Be sure to spout these back instantly or they will seem made up. Some examples:

  "No, they don't need to be any bigger! You're aerodynamic like this."
  "I know it gets you loud calls from construction workers, but it will pad your back from getting strained later in life."
  "It's not a hoof, honey. It's a conjoined toe, and you're beautiful just the way you are."
  "I wouldn't call it a beard; it's really more of a fu manchu."

- Sometimes, you won't be able to head this one off at the pass because it will come out of left field. A girl so beautiful she makes you want to weep tears of joy and semen that you've even gotten her naked will complain about her ass, which for all intents and purposes is perfect. When this happens, you shouldn't try to defuse the criticism. You should calmly get out of bed, get dressed, walk out the door, and never return. It doesn't matter if you were at your apartment. She can keep the lease. Anyone who's beautiful and still not happy with her appearance is obviously insane and should be avoided in a relationship. This kind of low self-esteem is like a gaping cold sore on her soul; you don't want to catch it.

QUICK TIP: Should your blind date be a member of a softball team, don't make a rude and ill-advised fat joke. Instead, be chivalrous. Excuse yourself, go to the bathroom, and tell the bathroom attendant to come check out this whale you harpooned.

Getting a Girl to Go Home

If you've ever had sex with an acquaintance, stranger, or enemy, you know that such intercourse causes one to feel an odd mix of triumph, self-loathing, and lubricant-greased fingers. At this point, whether you're a guy or a girl, the last thing you want is having that person spend the night. Then you've got to find her a toothbrush, see if she wants to borrow something to sleep in, worry about breakfast, and make a concerted effort not to wet the bed. Sex is supposed to be fun. That sounds like work. That said, you can't just throw your partner out on the street—you need at least to give off the impression that you're a considerate human being. Some do's and don'ts:

Don't: Say, "Thanks for the fuck—now get dressed," while throwing their clothes at them like you're playing some sort of demented game of dodgeball.

Do: Think ahead. Earlier in the evening, mention some vague reason you'll be getting up early in the morning. Usually saying you "have a thing . . . real early" is good enough. Nobody wants to wake up at the crack of dawn.

Don't: Buy a twin bed. While this dorm classic would keep overnight guests away, it happens to be an effective deterrent to real-world sex. On the plus side, though, you can get Smurf sheets on eBay.

Do: Offer to walk or drive the person home, or at least to her subway/bus stop. This way, you look considerate, but you still get rid of her. "Seriously, put your coat on, we're leaving. I am not letting you walk home alone. Right now."

Don't: Talk in your sleep. Sleep-talking is incredibly creepy and can scare a woman from ever speaking to you again.

Do: Snore. Serious girlfriends have to deal with snoring boyfriends all night long. In casual relationships, though, the girl almost always prefers to sleep in peace at home.

In Praise of the Larger Friend

Ahh, the fat friend. Every group of attractive females keeps one around to ensure that they themselves are not the token fugly at the bar. There are two ways you can identify who the fat friend is:

1. She's the one holding the sandwich. (No, you cannot have a bite.)

2. She's the one who is actually cool (thus keeping with the scientifically proven corollary that larger girls tend to have the best personalities since, unlike their hotter counterparts, they've actually been forced to cultivate them).

At this point, you're probably thinking to yourself, "WTF, fat girls aren't even real people. Why should I read about them, much less make conversation with them?" Because having the fat friend on your side is a huge (ha ha) asset when you try to hook up with her hotter friends, that's why.

First, a point of clarification: When we say "fat," we don't mean morbidly obese. Rather, we mean the girl who is a somewhat larger than her friends—probably because she drinks beer instead of Diet Coke with vodka, eats greasy food late at night instead of starving herself, and does less blow—but is significantly more enjoyable to hang out with for exactly these reasons. Fat Girl knows she's not the cat's meow in the looks department but is comfortable with it, which means she won't block your attempts to hook up with her hot friends (unlike Skinny Girl, who tends to be an insecure, jealous minx. The second you express interest in the hot friend of Skinny Girl, she'll do everything in her powers to ensure that you don't have a shot. Never confide in Skinny Friend). Fat Girl is good times, and she likes it when you have a good time. Which means if you guys have a good rapport, and if you're not a total fucking scumbag who's dicked over her friends before, she'll go out of her way to extend you a helping hand in the courtship process. She knows things your borderline-retarded guy friends don't have the faintest clue about. Should you call Jenny on Thursday or wait a few more days to avoid looking desperate? Do you have any shot whatsoever with Ali, or is she way the F out of your league? Fat Friend will offer up carefully reasoned responses peppered with insider info. It's like having a fleshy, jiggly cheat sheet.

So next time Fat Friend is at a bar being ignored, go over and buy her a beer. She's one of the best resources around.

Extremely Important Note: No matter how drunk you are, no matter how good an idea it might seem "just this once and we'll keep it a secret," you *must not* hook up with Fat Friend. This has nothing to do with her being fat and having your friends mock you for it (okay, maybe it has a little to do with her being fat). This girl is your greatest ally, but if you're always hanging out, she'll probably have at least some semblance of romantic interest in you. She knows you're out of her league, so she will be a good friend. However, if you get naked with her, she might start to get ideas. You'll have to defuse them, which means that you'll either hurt her feelings, lose your Fat Friend, or both. So show a little self-control and go to an all-night diner instead. She's always hungry.

Conclusion

You made it all the way to the end! Did you read every page carefully? You did? Jesus, were you not paying attention at all? All you really needed to do was skim through, pick out some important parts, and remember them! Oh, well, at least you learned a lot.